My Mother My Daughter

My Mother My Daughter

A Memoir

MARITA MALONE

Meine Mutter Meine Tochter, the German translation of this text, is available also on Kindle and in paperback.

Cover picture: painting of village, Minderlittgen, Germany, by H. Thomas, 1957.

First printing, 2015, Charleston
Second printing, 2016, Charleston

dedicated to Sofia, my sister

Contents

Acknowledgments

I have included brief stories throughout this book from an Old Lady as told to her by her father at bedtime. Most of these stories are derived from *Aesop's Fables*. Aesop, who lived circa 600 B.C., was once a slave. He had an uncanny ability to tell stories about animals. The fables always had morals. King Croesus of Lydia in Asia Minor freed him and promoted him to an ambassador, primarily because of his ability to persuade with words and stories. Unfortunately, Aesop could not dissuade a village from killing him, and he never documented his stories. It was not until 300 years later that someone compiled the fables that certainly had been altered some over time. Still, the spirit of his stories remains intact 2,600 years later. In Germany, octogenarians remember their parents telling stories to them about animals. These stories were an instrument for teaching right and wrong. I asked some old German women whether some of the fables in this book were similar to their childhood stories. Some of their stories are also in this book.

I also acknowledge Nancy Verrier (1991) for her words in *The Primal Wound: Understanding the Adopted Child*. She posits that adopted children who are severed early from their birth mother are often just as traumatized as older children who are separated. Verrier describes various characteristics that develop as a result of abandonment, and she uses a metaphor of a broken plate to explain relationships between a birth mother and child and an adoptive mother and child.

Finally, I acknowledge my editor and friend, Susan Cassidy, for her inspirational guidance.

Part One

One

FINDING THE KRYPTONITE

I slowly pan my bookcases. The walls and shelves are covered with pictures and certificates of appreciation from American presidents, prosecutors, directors, and foreign dignitaries, all nicely framed behind shining glass and addressed to Supervisory Special Agent Marita Malone. I have framed and mounted the personal letters from former U.S. Attorney Generals and Directors of the Federal Bureau of Investigations (FBI). They represent significant moments in my career. The plaques and letters map my transfers to major cities in the United States and assignments throughout the world, and attest that I worked and supervised hundreds of criminal, counterterrorism and counterintelligence cases. After the fall of the Berlin Wall, I went to Budapest to train Eastern Bloc law enforcement executives in democratic criminal justice techniques. After September 11, 2001, I was sent to Pakistan to train tribal princes to develop their own counterterrorism agency and major case management. I taught at the FBI Academy and three major universities. Among the mounds of political science and public administration, history, counterintelligence, security, and business and management books are my own published articles and book on managing law enforcement change. In the far corner of my office are dusty, dated English literature and history libraries and a couple of basketball and track books from when I was a high school teacher and winning basketball coach. Although my academic diplomas, certificates, and degrees are buried under my large, quirky collection of dining table place mats, I do not easily forget that I worked and paid for my high school private education, my undergraduate education, Master's and Doctorate of Philosophy degrees.

On top of one of the bookcases is a single sports trophy capped with a golden plastic male runner. I won third place in a five-mile run with a field of more than 100 men and only four women. As I accepted the award, the host apologized because the figure was not anatomically correct. He said, "We did not expect a woman to win."

They are the measures of my accomplishments. I can leap tall buildings in a single bound. Well . . . my admirers think I can.

But all that did nothing for me. I admit that the sports trophy makes me smile when I look at it, but most of the objects in my office elicit little to no emotion. There's a rolling marquee of plaques boasting my name, but I feel nothing when I notice them. I am fond of a few things, like the sweet china doll given to me by a now-deceased young friend that is a reminder of a kind, talented woman who could have been more. At eye level, facing the door is a small, plastic Looney Tunes "Marvin the

Martian" figure, his demonic white eyes set in a black spherical face. He's dressed in a Roman soldier's uniform with old-fashioned basketball shoes, a green, disk-like skirt, and a plume atop his helmet. Marvin holds an illudium Q-36 explosive space modulator, and he protects my office from dangerous intruders, such as my husband's cat and dog. In one of the barrister bookcases, in front of my Ayn Rand collection and a red hammer and sickle Soviet passport case, are seven hand-painted, nested Russian dolls, given to me by a Russian Jewish informant. I recall how he emigrated from the former Soviet Union, because, as a Jew, he was assured of having no opportunity for a good education or job.

Squeezed between the political science books are five small flag stems. The six by four-inch red, white and blue American flags are at attention. The flag that is yellowed, mended, and stapled to the thin pole was given to me when I became a United States citizen in 1956.

Across the room from the flags is my first piggy bank, a small Li'l Abner's "Can O' Coins" that my parents gave me in the 1950s. Filling that can was better than going to the neighborhood drug store to buy my favorite black licorice candy, because it meant a bus trip to downtown St. Louis with Mother. I loved watching the savings and loan employee pour the change out of L'il Abner's can into the loud change counter. The teller always greeted me with a big smile, and after completing the count, she took my savings book, used her adding machine to calculate the totals, and stamped it. While returning the book to me, she routinely said, "There you go, honey. You keep saving."

What's Wrong

My kryptonite, the Achilles heel of this superwoman, is also in my office — the Old Lady bookend. Holding up his end of the line of books is her husband, the Old Man, but he never speaks to me. Since I was a child, I have looked into the eyes of the Old Lady. There are times when she was my only companion. I imagined that she was a poor, old, matronly European woman, who worked time-unending in the fields. The Old Lady is a rather bulbous plaster figure, worn and battered by more than 70 years of supporting books and over 30 household moves. Small chips and abrasions in the plaster unjustly make her more scarred and her clothes more tattered than they were designed to be. Her round, yet chiseled face looks like a crumpled brown grocery bag. She has a permanent toothless grin.

The old woman sits on a stool buried somewhere beneath her skirts. Her neck and head are stooped forward and to the side; her back is straight and strong, as though she is sitting against a wall. Her tatty, long, forest green coat matches her scarf, tied in a knot under her protruding chin. A few wisps of mouse-gray hair escape the scarf. Her coat is parted in front and reveals her dirty beige apron and coal-black dress that cover her legs and ankles and meet the broken black ankle-tie shoes. She clutches a matching green bag that droops from her large, swarthy hand.

The plaster figure became my roommate when I was about six years old. My mother moved the bookend from her usual resting spot in the living room and put her on my chest of drawers. It was unusual to find the Old Lady and her male counterpart in my room. Why would a child want something so glum and old? At around that same time, I overheard my parents talking about a neighbor girl my age having an imaginary friend. I decided that since I did not have any friends, real or pretend, the Old Lady could serve the dual role. At first, I had one-sided conversations with her that were no more than giving voice to my inner thoughts. I usually talked about how I felt different from other kids. I wondered why I was never invited to parties, and why inside I was not feeling good. With her tilted head, and deep-set eyes staring into mine, I wondered, *surely she was listening to me.*

My first real conversation with the Old Lady took place when I was nine years old. It was late afternoon and I was lying across my bed, staring at the ceiling. Again, I was preoccupied with how different I seemed to be from other kids. Earlier that day I watched girls from my class stream into a neighboring house for a party. After the party started, I went into my bedroom, sat at my desk, and continued reading *Nancy Drew: The Hidden Staircase.* But my mind kept floating back to the neighbor's door opening in welcome to other girls, and I eventually fell onto my bed. Why wasn't I invited? I felt a painful weight growing on my chest. I pounded my chest with a fist, over and over, thinking it would alleviate the weight, release the pressure. The tightness felt like a heavy-weight wrestler pinning me to the mat, his knee to my chest. I could not wriggle free. My breathing, becoming shorter and shorter and more difficult to get, frightened me. I did not know then that I was living in emotional isolation. I felt that no one understood what I was going through, and, of course, that no one could help me.

The Old Lady speaks, "What's wrong, child?"
I glare at her intently. She speaks loudly, but with a speech
impediment similar to my own. I stop pounding my chest to see if
she would speak again. Nothing. I fix on her toothless grin. "Are you
making fun of me?" and then I fall asleep.

What's wrong?

I wanted the answer to the Old Lady's question. This seemingly innocent question would ultimately take me more than 50 years of searching to answer. My circuitous journey would be physical, mental and emotional. I would have to travel around the world, and deep within myself to find answers to and a solution for the oppressive weight that has been with me my entire life. The quest became my life . . . and my perception of what makes a happy ending would also change over the course of that life.

I made good choices and bad ones. The Old Lady was my companion throughout it all. She was my sounding board, my conscience and my confidante. Her eternal old age, sealed lips and deep-set eyes contained wisdom. She was the only one I dared talk to about anything that revealed a chink in my armor.

If I were to purge my office today, everything in it could go to the trash bin, except the Old Lady bookend. My journey with her has created something that is indeed "more powerful than a locomotive" — a life resolved. All my achievements were nothing more than mile markers along my journey to truth . . . to the answer to the Old Lady's question.

To get through this journey I taught myself two new languages. The first was the language of emotions, because I was not raised with any tools to understand my own heartbreak. I learned this language the hard way, by living. I learned it in order to know the right questions to ask, and to recognize that my hapless habit of constantly moving without a plan was a plan of sorts. And that "one foot in front of the other" ultimately gets one somewhere. The second language I learned was German, the language of my homeland.

Broken Rules

Before my quest for answers began, my life began. In 1950 Germany, only five years after the end of World War II, life had hardly returned to any level of normalcy. In the small villages, homes were still occupied by American soldiers, and food from the fields fed them first, and the native people second. That was the harsh reality of the war just fought and lost. The common people of Germany suffered through matters of policy not made by them. It was a time when families were broken all around Europe. People were trying to figure out how to forge a different future than the ones that they had originally imagined. A new world was coming, but it had not arrived yet. Survival was still paramount. And the Catholic Church ruled in many of these small villages. The war tore apart villages and families, but the pressures of religious and social morés were not any less intense. It was into this world that I would be born, a world where no one was particularly free, and women were even less so.

I was born in a tiny village of approximately 100 homes. Everyone knew everyone else's business. Though my birth mother had been married, her husband and father of her two children had been expelled from the country. She lived with her parents who denied her the right to join him in his homeland. What would follow was an intimate liaison with a neighbor. It is enough to imagine this time for my mother, a Catholic woman in a Catholic village, pregnant outside the confines of marriage. Regardless of her feelings for me, she lived in a village that was defined by gossip, judgment, disgrace, and the threat of damnation. If anything, people were less forgiving of such occurrences than before the war. Poverty and meager circumstances made even harsher realities for those who broke the rules.

My birth mother had broken the rules. My father broke the rules, too, but he didn't live daily with the consequences of his indiscretion. After three months of swimming through the daily sea of disapproval and shame, she gave me up to a Catholic orphanage. This was the first time I would feel the sharp edge of the knife that cuts away a human bond. After more than two years in that institution, I was cut loose again . . . this time from the home I knew – and the country of my birth. I was flown to the United States where I was adopted by an older American couple. I was too young to comprehend the enormity of what was happening to me.

Attitudes about adoption were different then. Little thought was given to the effects of such upheavals on the adopted children themselves. At the time there was a prevailing attitude that Americans were "saving" poor international children from tragic lives. In many cases they were. In hindsight, how does one compare the potential life as a "bastard" in a deeply religious, small, close-knit community with little opportunity for escape of any kind, to life as the legitimate member of an American family, with an opportunity for an education and freedom from toil in the field? Or should we be comparing growing up in a religious institution, such as the orphanage, and possibly joining the religious order, with few other prospects once one had outgrown the orphanage's safe confines, with life in a family, in America, free from stigma and want?

Isn't life more than opportunity and education? Isn't life about bonds and connections and having a home in someone's heart? Things happen to a child who is uprooted, severed from her mother, then uprooted again, and then again. One learns how to survive, if not how to thrive. In my first six years of life, I spent three months with my birth mother, almost three years in an orphanage, two years in my adoptive home, then a year in kindergarten at boarding school with children at least six years older than I. Then, I returned home for seven years before leaving again to live with my adoptive grandmother and the Catholic boarding school. After the age of 13, I never returned to my adopted family's home for anything more than a long weekend.

This is the foundation of my life. These experiences created the girl alone in her room, pounding on her chest to relieve the pain that threatened to crush her. These facts of my life led to my becoming the girl who needed to talk to someone, even if to the Old Lady bookend that stood on her dresser. And those conversations, coupled with the oppressive weight on my chest, led to the journey with the qualified happy ending.

Two

Hiding Out

The Privilege of Privacy

E very day, as a young girl, I walked alone along the major thoroughfare between our tired, four-room, white stucco bungalow and the school. The gray front porch reached across two-thirds of the house, but it bowed like the back of an old gray mare. Built in 1927, it was one of those houses that are longer than they are wide. Although our home was not quite a shotgun house, we had to go through one room to get to another. There were no hallways. When my brother and I came into our parents' lives, my father, a small but strong, stocky man, added a master bedroom. He converted the back porch into a bedroom minus heat ducts, which became my brother's room. To get to my parents' bedroom from our front door, we went from the living room, through the dining room, my bedroom, and into their bedroom. Going through my bedroom seemed to be the only way to get anywhere in the house.

Our family shared one bathroom with no shower. Eventually, my handy father added a shower and toilet to the unfinished basement. Only he used it regularly because that space was also home to the house's plumbing, loose electrical wires, the coal storage area, spider webs and creepy crawlers. For a child, it was a dark, chilling experience to go into that basement. I never knew when the coal monster would throw open the coal storage door with a blast from the fiery furnace, or when the spider webs would wrap my face in an invisible claw. I imagined spiders crawling up through the toilet, and snakes coming up through the drain of the concrete shower. I avoided it whenever I could.

We lived in Ferguson, Missouri, one of the original suburbs in the Midwest, on a busy street with bungalows that were turned into storefront homes. Our house shared the block with a Veterans of Foreign Wars chapter, a used car lot, a barbershop, an insurance agency, and the residence of a bunny girl from Hugh Hefner's Playboy Club, which eventually became another small business. On the other side of the bunny girl lived Mr. and Mrs. Amen, an elderly, proper couple. The wife was nicknamed Mrs. Crabapple by us kids because of her crabby nature. We were always doing something that irritated her; we unintentionally stepped on her grass or batted a ball into her backyard, or set up squirrel traps in the pear tree. We shared the telephone party line with them, making it very easy for Mrs. Amen to pick up the phone and complain to my parents. My brother and I surreptitiously listened in on her conversations with the police about us. Next to the Amens were the Kellers, who had a boat-load of children. In addition to the noises of the street, the commercial airplanes that landed at the nearby major airport frequently interrupted our conversations, shook our small house, and precariously moved trinkets on our tabletops.

Our home was comfortable enough, albeit very humble. My father worked hard for little money, but we were never without the staples. With the exception of my brother's bedroom, the family always had heat in the winter and food on the table. Out of necessity we developed the habit of frugality and ate "day-old" bread and cheap cuts of meat on Eagle-stamp plates with Betty Crocker-stamp flatware. We ate whatever was deeply reduced in price, including pig's snout, cow tongue, and buffalo catfish directly from the tainted Mississippi River. Sometimes the meat was so tough that I spent what seemed like an eternity trying to chew it. At some meals, I could not get past chewing to move onto the next fork full of food. I took to excusing myself to the bathroom, where I spit the mutilated piece into the toilet, and flushed it away. After a while, my parents caught on and stopped allowing me to go to the bathroom during dinner. Instead, I learned to swallow whole chunks of gristle meat.

We bought used cars that had already seen better days. One of our cars looked like it had survived several wars. After years of direct sunlight, the 1955 formerly deep red Ford station wagon was more of a faded tomato cream soup with rusted out wheel wells and fenders. When my father drove, I dizzily watched the gray road race by beneath the floorboards.

Our clothes were always new or home sewn by my father's sister. My seamstress aunt, whose prime had been during the 1930s Depression and whose sense of style remained rooted firmly in that era, made my dresses. I could easily have passed for a black and white picture in a history book. Though well intentioned, these old fashioned clothes did nothing to help me feel like other girls my age. By the time I was in fifth grade, I fought wearing the dresses altogether. My mother scolded, "You can't wear jeans to church."

"Why not?" I objected.

"Because I said so."

Having no response to that — and no say in the matter — I tried other ploys. I regularly complained of a stomach ache or a fever, although the latter never worked because it required verification with a thermometer stuck under my tongue. I would huff really hard, hoping that extra heat from my lungs would throw the thermometer above 98.6 degrees Fahrenheit. Science was never my strong suit. My embarrassment continued until late in high school when a high school roommate passed down a store-bought, sleeveless summer dress that was a deliberately faded pink design on white. I wore that dress, regardless of the season, until I could afford to buy another, in-style dress.

We were a family of four, but my brother, John, and I played with families in the neighborhood who lived in nursery rhyme homes — small houses, big families and hard working parents. We played with one poor family that had six children, and another family with eight children. Often as John and I walked the short cut to one of their homes, through a weedy field and across a tree log over the creek, I recited the nursery rhyme:

There was an old woman who lived in a shoe.
She had so many children, she didn't know what to do ....

Because we were distracted by something in the creek bed, most of the time I did not get very far in the rhyme. The creek was an endless source of entertainment when we had nothing to do. We balanced carefully as we walked on the sewer pipes across the waterway. We dared each other not to scoot across the really skinny ones. It gave us days and days of exploration. Eventually, though, the creek became a taker. Jimmy Oligschlaeger, my classmate, was exploring when the creek flooded and the turbulent waters took him all the way into the river. After that, the creek became evil and dark.

Most times when we eventually arrived at the shoe house, all eight children were sitting around an early 1950s black-and-white television with aluminum foil-covered rabbit-ear antennae and grainy picture. Their mother was always in the kitchen surrounded by food, wrappers and dishes on the table and counters. Their house was much smaller than ours, and they were living on an even shorter shoestring than we.

I was always self-conscious about our scrimping and "making do." Despite seeing other families in our neighborhood do the same, I didn't compare my family to them. I compared my family to those living in wealthier neighborhoods. They had more. We had less. Other families had single-party telephone lines and whole-house air conditioning. We afforded a window air conditioner that was strategically located in the center of the house — my bedroom. When the air conditioner was on, I could not close either of my doors. Initially, on extremely hot days, my brother and father slept in my 10 x10-foot bedroom with me. The window air conditioner became so popular that my parents eventually moved a sofa, TV-dinner tray tables, the television set and other furniture into my bedroom. Often the whole family stayed in my bedroom, which became the family room, the dining room, and even the dormitory. When it was time to clean, mine was a room where there was more dusting than mopping.

I cried and pleaded for my privacy and something to call my own, but my parents kept moving more furniture and people into my room. I begged to switch bedrooms with my brother, even though my room was the larger and cooler room, but my parents said no.

"Excuse me. Poor people have poor ways. Your parents are struggling to make ends meet," defends the Old Lady. "Privacy is a privilege. It's a mid-20th century concoction. As I child I was one of seven children living in three rooms. In the barn, behind the pigs was my escape. I never asked for privacy, and my children never asked for privacy."

"Perhaps you had nothing to hide. I hide my thoughts because I don't know how to say them, or what people will think once I say them. The emotions build up until I feel trapped in my body."

Even as I speak, I feel uncomfortable sharing this with my only companion. What do I have to hide? I am not sure.

"*You're too small to be left with your baffling notions. Besides, that's not all you want. You're antsy, like you're looking for something. What is it?*" *The Old Lady is relentless.*

I sass back, "I don't think I'd be talking to you, if I had known what I was looking for."

"*Which is it: privacy or alone time? There's a big difference. Privacy is when a person doesn't want to be observed or disturbed. I never had that. Alone time is more like solitude, which I had when I worked in the fields. It was a time when my body cultivated the potatoes and my mind cultivated my thoughts. My mind was a sanctuary, a place of refuge and safety. I was withdrawn inside my head. At the end of the day I walked back to the village, dirty, tired, and somewhat wiser. You, on the other hand, seem to want to escape more than anything else."*

I repeat her words. "I want my mind to be a sanctuary, a place of refuge and safety. I want to be withdrawn within my head."

The sunlight flashes over the Old Lady's face. "You don't want privacy or alone time. You want a retreat for when things are uncomfortable for you. Better yet, you want a hideout."

She pauses for a second. Then she says, as though a second flash of light struck her, "You're ashamed of your parents, aren't you?"

In My Mother's Camp

I *was* ashamed of my parents. They were almost 50 years older than I. When I tried to figure out the reason for my loneliness . . .

my lack of friends . . . for my feeling different, my youthful logic said that it had to be my old parents and our humble house. They must be to blame for my not fitting in . . . for the weight on my chest.

A few years ago, when I asked my brother, also adopted, about his memories, he said without hesitation, "Going to Dr. Judy."

"Why? Were you sick?" I asked.

"No. I was circumcised. The orphanage in Germany didn't take care of that."

Too much information for a sister, but I asked anyway, "How old were you when you had the procedure?"

"Maybe four or five years old."

I asked impishly, "Did it hurt? Did they use a large bandage or a tiny band aid?"

"Not funny. The other things that I remember are that we were poor, and our parents were old."

So . . . we were both embarrassed.

However, if they were the only two issues of my childhood, they might have complicated things, but they were not the cause of the oppressive weight on my chest.

When I think of my mother, I see her in the kitchen — a distorted version of June Cleaver, that perfect 1950s television mother: a lean figure trussed in a dress and apron, sensible, worn Women's Army Corp (WAC) shoes with two-inch heels, and nylons that were secured above the knee with garters. Unlike Mrs. Cleaver, she had no pearls. She was an attractive enough woman with a sharp, pointy nose. It seemed she always wore a scowl privately, and a laugh publicly. She had long bird-like legs and, when scowling, her pointy nose looked more like a beak. I remember once, after playing outside and getting muddy, going inside to a very angry mother and being sent to my room to change my clothes. I remained there until my father returned from work. While waiting to face the music, I drew a picture of my mother with a human torso, a bird head and bird legs. The picture was insignificant, except for that scowl and the look in her eyes. I do not remember a single time when the two of us were together unaccompanied that she did not wear that countenance.

> *"That's not a very flattering picture of your mother," the Old Lady says.*
>
> *"It is what I see when I think of my mother. Her scowl is particularly harsh when she's disappointed in me. I'm not what she had hoped for."*
>
> *"I expect you to be more reverent, someone who shows respect," she scowls. I do not like that look because it reminds me of my mother, but I don't cringe; I feel warmth for the Old Lady.*
>
> *I whisper, "It's not that I am disrespectful. I am afraid of her."*

I recall one of our family dinners. While I don't remember my offense, I remember her response vividly. In a flash, my mother jerked away from the table and headed for me with her arm raised to strike. Her glaring eyes bore through me. In a reflex-ive move, I threw my arms up to protect my head, conscious only of the blows I was trying to prevent. I was unaware that I still held a sharp cooking fork, and when my mother struck, her hand was impaled on it. She screamed in pain and jumped away lightning fast. The kitchen descended into a scene of chaos, with chairs flying back, and my brother, father, mother and I all bumping into each other. The dog ran to the safety of a corner. My father wrapped towels around her hand to stop the bleeding, and they hurried out the door to go to the hospital.

"Stay here!" my father barked, as he slammed the front door behind them. I began to sniffle, out of fear of punishment, certainly. But my tears were largely because I felt like a terrible person. It did not matter that she was going to hit me. It did not matter that it was an accident brought on by trying to block her blows. It did not matter that I was scared of Mother. It only mattered that I did this horrible thing.

"Now you've done it," said John, as he held the quaking dog.

Later in grade school, Mother and I tangled again, over another long forgotten offense. She charged me in the dining room and grabbed my hair with both hands and started to pull and push me. My hands clasped over hers, and I pressed them hard against my head, in hopes to lessen the painful pull. We danced in angry circles as I tried to get loose.

I screamed, "Let go! Let go!"

My father, who was in the basement, heard me screaming, and he ran to the source of the noise. "Let her go!" but the deep-voiced demand fell on deaf ears. Finally, after trying to disengage the two of us, he pushed Mother to the floor. As she was falling, she released my hair. "Go to your room!" he ordered me, as he glared at Mother on the floor. I followed his orders, but I was angry that he might have hurt my mother. An eerie quiet hung over the house for the next couple of days. My mother said nothing during that time, but I knew that she was indignant. That incident set the tone for the rest of our lives as mother and daughter.

I had my faults, especially for those times. I was a tom boy. I loved to climb trees, wrestle, play baseball, and hunt rabbits with the .22 rifle — all the things that boys did. I jumped over wide creeks and sometimes missed, stuck my finger in bicycle spokes to stop the spin of the wheel. I did whatever it took to get applause.

A neighborhood child visited and talked about eating fried eggs: "My parents eat fried eggs every morning. I hate them, because they are so runny and yucky, especially when they get cold."

Gloating, I said, "Oh, they are just raw." I did not know that fried eggs were not the same as raw eggs. I knew fried eggs came directly from the refrigerator and out of the shell. I also did not know that they were cooked; why would anyone cook something as runny as fried eggs? The neighbor kid told me I did not know what I was talking about, and taunted me, "I betcha you can't eat a raw egg." Challenge on. Without giving a second thought I went into the house with the neighbor and into the refrigerator, cracked the top of the raw egg, and sucked it out. It took only a drop to comprehend my mistake, but to save face I drank the rest of it. After the initial taste, I turned my back to the neighbor, which allowed me the time and privacy to close my eyes and focus on not throwing up as the slime eased down my throat.

Later, my brother dared me, "Betcha can't eat an ant sandwich." I marched into the house, grabbed a piece of white Bunny bread, marched back outside, and scooped up black ants with my thumb and index finger and sprinkled them onto the bread, again closed my eyes, and ate them.

Hardly a week went by that I did not have a new injury -- a scrape on the knee, a torn finger that needed stitches, or sunburns with large blisters that made it unbearable to wear a shirt. Wearing a towel on my shoulders with no shirt became my signature around the house, until I learned to wear t-shirts under my swimming suits, which was unfashionable, even for me. Eventually, swimming pools became the enemy, and I stayed away from them. Two weeks before my First Communion, my mother grounded me because she did not want me to be in a delicate white dress and veil with cuts, black eyes, and bruises. I remember Mother ending her lecture, ". . . and don't climb the pear tree."

The neighborhood kids, and sometimes my brother, occasionally received a dose of my tomboyism. Once when my grandmother was babysitting us, she came outside to tell us not to get dirty. The neighbor boy, Freddie, casually said, "Wow, she's old." Faster than I could say, "She is *not*," I punched him in the face, and blood spurted from his nose. After that, Freddie was not allowed to visit our house. On another occasion, John and I were playing "cowboys" in the house, and I took the butt of a toy handgun and knocked out part of one of his front teeth. My father was seething; like a run-away train, he collected every toy bow, arrow, rifle and handgun, and threw them all into the trash. It was a sad day for cowboydom.

Once when my mother's sister and three adult nieces knocked on our door for a scheduled visit, I answered the door and asked, "Hello, when are you leaving?" Obviously they did not fit into my schedule that day, and I did not possess the social graces to pretend they did. I was a motivated tomboy in jeans. My mother and father probably expected their children to be "seen" but not "heard," and my brother seemed to fit that model more than I. Mother was hoping I would be like the 17th century Baroque children's portraits, children's faces and statures in adult clothes with adult demeanors. My mother's vision of what I should be -- quiet, cute, and malleable -- I was not.

Aloof, however, I was good at.

The Old Lady sits in silence for a while, and eventually says, "Is your mother frustrated with you? You seem like a handful." The Old Lady does not give me a chance to defend myself. ". . . And parents, like children, live and learn. You're too critical of your mother, and clearly you two are not in the same camp. How old are you now, child?""

"Twelve, old enough to realize that I am only a child, and things between my mother and me are awkward. My mother hasn't made an effort to understand who I am. I want to know why I feel like a space invader in this house."

"And what exactly does 'space invader' mean? My grandchild talks about aliens all the time, but they are people from outer space. Too much television, I think . . . ," the Old Lady rambles.

This time I cut her off. "I don't fit into this house. It's not that the house is small, but that when I look at our family photos, I see 2 + 1 + 1. I should see a family, four people but one family."

"Ohhh, you meant the word alienated." She thinks. "But you never went into your mother's camp."

"Should I?" I begin to fidget with the stuff on my desk. I look around and see a crooked picture that needs straightening, and a dust bunny on the floor that must be captured. "I am only a child, but am I selfish for not being able to enter my mother's world, for not being whatever she wishes and hopes for?" I feel the growing pressure on my chest. The wrestler that had pinned me down earlier has grown to the size of a sumo wrestler. Almost breathless, "Shouldn't my mother come into my camp instead?"

"At first, yes, but eventually you must invite her into your life and go into her camp. She is older, and she seems to struggle. Her dream of a husband and family is probably not working out exactly as she had expected, like someone else I know," as her vacuous eyes latch onto mine." Maybe your mother had unrealistic expectations and doesn't know how to deal with them."

I must be uncharacteristically preoccupied with the cleanliness of my room, because the only thing I really hear are her last words, "You don't understand what I am saying, do you?"

The Old Lady does not wait for an answer. She continues, "When I was a child, my father used to tell us short stories from Aesop. It was his way of trying to form us. Almost every night when all the children were in bed, he would come into our room with a single candle and a worn book. He would tell us a story about animals, and then make us guess what the moral of the story was. We rarely got it right, but it was fun. One of the stories was about this dog in the manger who took a nap in the ox's bed. The ox returned from a long day of work, entered his stall, and saw the dog. The dog was angry because he was awakened. When the ox went to eat the hay, the dog snapped at him. So, the ox could neither rest nor eat, and the dog was not resting or eating. Eventually the patient ox said to the dog, 'If you want to eat my hay and sleep in my stall, go ahead, but you do neither, and you will let me do neither. That seems rather bad-mannered and ill-natured.' Perhaps you and your mother are the dog. You are both disappointed about your way of life, and both are ill-natured. "The Old Lady then whispers, "I am sad for you, child; you are so serious, so worn-out, and at such a young age."

I stare again at the Old Lady's empty brown eyes, thinking that her existence is probably more isolated than mine. As if she were reading my mind, she says, "My loneliness comes with old age and experience, from suffering that came from a life time. I lived through two devastating wars, the deaths of family and long-time friends. I lived through crop failures that led to starvation and scurvy. I am old, toothless and penniless. I live my old age completely removed from the here and now. I am on this world, but not in it. As old people grow older, they become more detached from the world, less and less part of it. Two simple things are important to them daily coffee and cake, and chit chat that does not disturb their memories. For me, my arthritis is a daily reminder of my loneliness and suffering. You, on the

other hand, have only begun to live. Your painful reminder of
your loneliness is the weight on your chest."

    I do not understand what she said, but I stop fidgeting.

    "And you'll never go into her camp, because you are afraid of
her. You avoid what you fear, and because you avoid the things you
fear, you can't learn more about them."

Say Nothing

When my brother John and I were in grade school, we often played together. He was a curious, curly-headed kid who
quietly moved about. Our summers were spent exploring the
creek, bicycling to the drug store and town park, playing bad-
minton and baseball in the backyard, climbing over fences,
throwing rotten pears at each other, and strategically setting
up the little green plastic soldiers. John spent every cent of
his allowance and anybody else's money, with which he could
abscond, on military airplane models. He snookered me into
giving him my 50-cents-a-month allowance. Our parents did
not want him to spend so much time and money on models,
and eventually my brother felt compelled to hide the models
in the doghouse.

    John's intelligence was remarkable, and his curiosity turned
unintentionally destructive. As a young teen, he was curious
what heat could do to concrete. He took my father's blowtorch
and aimed for the basement concrete floor. He was awed at how

the heat from the blowtorch exploded the concrete into bits the size of drinking coasters. After creating about 10 of those "coasters" and their holes, he stopped. While taking high school chemistry, he was intrigued with the combustion of potassium permanganate crystals and glycerin. The flames were intense and its quick work of burning through steel was impressive. At the end of the school day he jumped on the school bus and used the steel bus floor for his experiment. He was in the back of the bus surrounded by his classmates, and within seconds he demonstrated an incredible fireworks and quick job of another coaster-sized hole, only this time in the bus flooring. The hole added a new dimension to his rides from school as he observed the passing road under his feet. In his increasing desire to know how things functioned, he took apart our parents' electrical devices, vehicles, and other intriguing items that had parts, but he could not return them whole. All the *Popular Mechanics* and *Popular Electronics* magazines in the world could not put them back together again.

My brother's curiosity did not endear him to my father. Daddy returned home daily from work, tie loosened at the collar, feet dragging across the floors to the back bedroom. He routinely removed his skinny tie, detachable collar, silk shirt that his sister made from World War II parachutes, and his baggy trousers. He changed into jeans and began cooking for the family. After dinner, he washed the dishes, and I dried them. Daddy eventually deployed to fix my brother's mistakes: the radio that John could not reassemble after taking it apart, the concrete floor, and the side of the house that John acciden-tally hit with a car that he was not licensed to drive. He also addressed chores that my brother decided did not peak his in-terest. Then, he would go to the basement and iron clothes or fiddle among his tools. He was a carpenter, electrician, plumb-er, furniture maker, mechanic, boiler maker, farmer, hunter, fisherman, musician, and an artist. In an odd way, my father was a Renaissance man.

John was our father's primary recipient of corporal punish-ment. (Actually, this arrangement worked in my favor.) Eventually my brother had just one chore, to feed the pet dog, and he did not do that very well. We were playing in the yard with Pal, when our father popped out of the house,

"John, come here!"

In a quick whisper to him, I blurted, "Did you feed the dog?"

"I forgot."

"Uh-oh."

No more words were spoken, but Daddy charged my brother with his arm and hand raised, and Pal jumped in the fray and took a chunk from my father's arm. My brother got out of feeding the dog again because my father had to be rushed to the hospital emergency room to get stitches in his arm. Generally, Daddy believed my brother was lazy.

My brother's strongest dislike was reserved for the family farm. Some of the land was rented to the neighboring farm-ers for their cows to graze, and some was share-cropped. The log cabin, where we stayed for weekends and longer, was built in 1792. It did not have electricity, in-door plumbing, or any modern conveniences. The cabin had two main rooms, the kitchen and the living room. In the latter was a colossal hearth. In the former was a large 1880s cast iron wood burning cooking stove. Perhaps the original owners had slept upstairs, which was one large attic room, but the stairs to the attic were steep, and the attic was already inhabited by wasps, bees and black snakes that took exception to anyone who attempted to climb beyond the first two steps. In the late 1800s, an addition was added to the log cabin, but it needed a lot of repair by the time that we bought it.

So, too, the fences around the house, chicken coop, barn yard and outhouses were in shambles, and much of the landscape needed to be cleared. The chicken coop, old barn, tool sheds, and pig sty were made of wood slats that grayed and bent, and the roofs were weather-curled, rusted tin. The only inhabitants were the cities of wasps and hornets and an occasional migrant bird, except in the old log corn bin, which also housed garden snakes. The newest building was the 40-year old white slatted wood barn, the loft which we rented out for the neighbor's hay. My brother and I romped among the hay bales. Only I was covered with jiggers the following day. I scratched until I drew blood.

Daddy worked tirelessly at the farm. Mother stayed close to the cabin. I jumped in with my father and worked outdoors. I enjoyed cutting the acres of weeds, pulling down old fences, painting the out buildings, repairing the metal roofs, using the sickle and scythe for clearing, and planting hundreds of evergreens, fruit and nut trees. I loved sweating; it was a sign of accomplishment.

My brother, on the other hand, despised sweating. He was more cerebral. His questions were quirky: "If a turtle loses its shell, is it naked or homeless?" "What was the best thing since sliced bread?" "Why is it that night falls and day breaks?"

In that same adult conversation with my brother about how he remembered our childhoods, his remembrance of Daddy contrasted mine. As a child, I looked upon him as a protector who was willing to teach me "substantive," versus domestic, things, such as how to shoot a rifle and shotgun, mow fields of weeds with a large garden tractor, drive nails with a hammer, and use other tools to build and tear down.

On one occasion when playing in the fields, John and I meandered where the neighbor's cattle were grazing. In the same field was a pond that was one of two water sources for the cattle. We approached the embankment, drawn by the "ribbit, ribbit" of the bull frogs, and then realized that we had about 10 pairs of large brown eyes staring at us. My brother looked at me wide-eyed without saying a word, but with fear written all over his face. I, being more interested in the frogs, said absent-mindedly, "Afraid of frogs?" He pointed at the other kind of, albeit attentive, bull and cows. Then, without a word, he took off running in the direction from which we had come. I heard and then felt the earth shudder and realized, "Holy Cow, we're being charged! Wait for me!" I cried. But, my brother was gone. I dropped the stick that I had used to terrorize the frogs and took off behind John. He was already shinnying himself up an old oak tree, and by the time I was at the tree, the bull was on my heels. I depended on my brother, who was a year older than I, to have mercy on me and pull me up to the first branch. It was not a pretty rescue, but as I was scrambling onto the first branch, my brother grabbed me by the seat of my pants and hoisted me. The tree was circled by these 1,500-pound creatures shuffling in place, staring at us. My buttocks dangled from a limb, but it was high enough to avoid a steer's horns. By then, our father heard the ruckus and ran into the field to call off the cattle. He gave a loud, deep, indiscernible command, and the cattle obeyed; bumping into each other, they retreated to the pond. We scrambled down the tree, and I forced my little girl legs to run fast to my father's side. There, standing next to him, I felt safe, but the feeling did not last long because gave us chores to keep us out of trouble.

My brother believed Daddy was toxic. Our father had a temper, but I do not remember that. In our adult conversations, John said, "Don't you remember Daddy spending all his time in the basement?" That I do remember, but it is one of those memories that I worked on forgetting.

"Yeah," my brother added, "He went to the basement to escape from Mother. He drank down there." I did not ask John how he knew that, and I did not tell him how I knew. More than once as a child, curious to see what Daddy was doing in the basement, I tiptoed through the kitchen, and at the top of the basement steps, I lay on my stomach, looking into the basement. I watched him in his blue-striped robe, tinkering at the tool bench, ironing, or washing his hands. As he moved about the basement, he would grab a bottle of either whiskey or scotch and drink from it. When I needed to talk to him, I deliberately made a lot of noise in the kitchen before I pointedly clomped down the stairs. Facing him, I smelled liquor on his breath, and looked away, as though my looking away would help him disguise his breath. Eventually, I decided that when my father was downstairs, the basement was off limits. When Mother asked me to get something from the basement or cellar, I was more willing to risk her wrath than to see my father in his robe.

"Speak, Old Lady." I wait.

Eventually, the Old Lady starts telling another one of her fables. "The lion, the king of beasts, was told by his mate that his breath stunk. The lion king did a lot of roaring to show everyone that he still was king. The lion first asked the sheep whether his breath stunk, and the sheep thought the lion wanted the truth, but the sheep lost her head to the lion. The wolf came along and saw the sheep's carcass. The lion asked the wolf if his breath were foul. The wolf told the king that his breath smelled like sweet blossoms in the spring, and the king killed him because he did not want flattery. Finally, the fox arrived, and he pretended to have a cold. 'Sorry, King, but I have such a head cold that I cannot smell at all.' Child, you have a particularly dangerous memory, and if I am at all wise, I should say nothing. When you decide to deal with your father's actions, I will talk with you."

"Hmm, I rarely think about his drinking."

John's other memory of my father was on his 17th birthday. My father and brother were in the backyard, and he hit my brother, again. But this time, John said to Daddy, "Thanks for the birthday gift." John ended his memory with, "He never hit me again, but I never gave him another chance." After that last hit, John was rarely seen at home.

My mother's favoritism for my brother was not disguised. She was old school, and she expected John to be successful, and therefore did what it took to help her son. Although she seemed content with being a housewife, she took a job with the federal government so that John could continue to go to a private, all-boys grade school. When I was in eighth grade, my father, who must have understood my jealousy, apologized that he could not afford the same education for me that my brother was getting. John went on to a prestigious all-boys high school.

When I was about ten years old, I lay in bed wishing I were a boy instead of a girl. Boys seemed to have more independence, more opportunities, and did not always have to be picked for the girlish game "Red Rover" or other teams. If I were a boy, I would not have to worry about the parties I was never invited to or whether I was pretty or if my hair looked nice, or if I had the most recent fashions or popular friends. If I were a boy, my mother would like me. I cannot help but think of the Old Lady's dog in the manger story.

I got up from bed and locked myself in the bathroom. I stared into the mirror. I had carrot red hair with unfashionable bangs and pigtails, light eyebrows, two vampire-like lateral incisor teeth, white porcelain skin with freckles, and I wore light blue metal glasses. I was envious of the other girls who were invited to parties and had girlfriends with whom they listened to 45-RPM records and practiced the newest dances. I hummed Chubby Checker's Twist and started dancing, all the while staring at myself in the mirror. A loud knock at the door and my mother's harsh command startled me, and I jumped to the sink to run the water, as though I was washing my hands.

My brother befriended Freddie, and I tried hanging around with them, but my fist in his face ended that. My best friend, other than the Old Lady, was my used "girl" bike that I painted forest green and white. It had the fat tires and the s-shaped bar that allowed girls to delicately get onto the bike. I rode and rode and rode — alone. Eventually, I put a basket on the front of the bike and multi-colored streamers on the handlebars. But I grew discontented because other girls my age had new racer bikes. My own brother had a new, midnight blue racer bike. I felt slightly betrayed by him.

On a steamy summer day in our preteens, John and I walked along the railroad tracks behind our house, and we decided to derail a train by putting some small stones on the rails. The scorching heat was all but forgotten as we set upon our mission. Out of nowhere we heard a deep, God-like voice from above: "What do you think you're doing?" Startled, we looked up the small incline. The sun was directly in our eyes, and this dark apparition was ominous. A police officer was staring down at us. Who knows what we said, but the officer gave us a ride to our home.

As the police officer marched us up the front steps of our home, Mother's glowering eyes and scowl met us. The police officer and our mother whispered back and forth, and the next thing I knew I was sent to bed. I was sure Mother was planning to send me to prison. First, I stab her with a fork; then I say or do something awful enough that she wanted to pull out all my hair; and now the police officer is at the door. I looked around my bedroom to see what I could take with me to prison. Nothing, save my friend, the Old Lady. I started planning my escape from the house, but I had no one to go to. My mind slipped into the Old Lady's world, but not for long. I was brought back to reality when I heard the kitchen cupboard door slam. While I envisioned how I would look in a black and white striped suit, John was in the kitchen eating a peanut butter sandwich.

Taking a Lifetime

At the same time that I started feeling the building pressure on my chest, I started snooping around the house. When my parents left for grocery shopping or a meeting, and my brother was gone doing whatever brothers do, I had at least two routines. First and always, I raided the flat white freezer chest in the cellar. It was not that I was hungry, but I had a sweet tooth that required constant feeding. As soon as the house was empty, I was in the cellar checking the inventory. The Merita brownies and the ice cream were my primary targets. On numerous occasions, I brought a large spoon with me to the basement, leaned over the edge of the large freezer, and ate ice cream out of the box. When the box of ice cream was at the very bottom of the freezer, it was all the strength I could muster to keep the last third of my body from falling into the locker. I knew that I had been discovered when I went downstairs to sneak some dessert, and a big padlock had been installed on the lid.

My second pastime while home alone was to play Mother's old 78-RPM glass records: "The Elephant Walk," and the classical composers, such as Rossini, Chopin, Mendelssohn, and Puccini. I cranked up the sound as loud as I could. Listening to Rossini's finale of the *William Tell Overture* filled me with energy. Sometimes it put me in the mood to do my chores.

On one Saturday, with the music loud enough to reach Mrs. Amen's ears, I decided to do a particularly thorough job of dusting. I had seen a spray can labeled Rose Petal Silver in the pantry, and I decided that the contents would create a brilliant sheen on the furniture. I sprayed the unblemished, mahogany television set, and out came a burst of tiny silver speckles. I returned to the pantry to get a duster to rub the chemical into the wood, but by the time I returned to the scene of the crime the chemical was permanently adhered in a thousand silver pin-like dots. Ahem, the chemical did not dissolve. I stopped acting like a conductor of the Overture and turned off the record player. Minutes later my parents returned, and my father's antenna that searches for what's not right in the house s immediately honed in on the silver spots on the television. I was sent to my room. I sat there feeling terrible — no, worse, I was crucifying myself -- for destroying the mahogany television. What our family had was not expensive, but it was clean, well-cared for, and hard earned.

I learned to appreciate classical music by listening to those old records over and over. The records were scratched badly before I began to play them, but by the time I was finished with them, the music was hard to distinguish, except in my mind. I learned to enjoy the soothing melodies, albeit dramas, of the Romantic Period. Listening to those records, except for Rossini's *William Tell Overture*, became a source of peace and tranquility. Later, listening to Puccini's and Tchaikovsky's works became an elixir for the weight on my chest. I never allowed myself to forget what I did to the television set, though, because Bugs Bunny's charge and the Lone Ranger's call to his horse, "Hi-ho, Silver," was followed by the finale of the *William Tell Overture*, the same music that had bedeviled me into using Rose Petal Silver.

The third thing I did when everyone else was away from the house became an obsession. I routinely scoured the house for things that might make me feel better. My parents had mostly fiction books on the living room shelves, but I saw two old hardbound non-fictions, one on anatomy, and the other on physiology, which I tried to read. Of course, the diagrams helped me make sense of the otherwise incomprehensible words. When I was in fifth grade, I studied the books more earnestly by outlining the text in them. It was a pastime. I sat at my drop front secretary desk, which my father had built from a chest of drawers, with one foot on the chair rung to allow my knee to prop up the weak supports of the writing surfaces. I slouched over the books, my faced pressed within six inches of the print. I accumulated piles of useless outlines. For a Christmas gift, my parents gave to me the Invisible Woman, a clear plastic, naked woman with removable, color-coated body parts.

The gift gave me an idea for my first investigative test and anatomy experiment: how much does each of my body parts weigh? When my parents were out of the house, I moved the bathroom scale onto the relatively spacious kitchen floor. I readied with a pencil and paper and lay on the floor. I laid my head on the scale, and documented 40 pounds. Then one finger - three pounds. A hand - 10 pounds. A leg - 50 pounds, and so on. By the time I added the weights of all the body parts, I weighed more than 300 pounds. My experiment was a failure, because when I stood on the scale, I weighed 70 pounds. My weaknesses in science and mathematics prevailed throughout my life.

During one of my snooping expeditions, I found a small green 1953 publication entitled *Ink Link*, a news magazine from my father's employer. It was on one of the living room end tables' shelves, stashed under the archdiocesan Catholic Church weekly papers, the church bulletins and the *TV Guide*. One of the articles had a picture of my parents and John and me, barely four and three years old, respectively, in front of a Christmas tree in our living room. I read the words around the photo. Unlike the physiology and anatomy books, I understood most of these words. My brother and I were adopted from Germany. We were classified as war orphans, but I already knew that. My parents never kept that information from us. But now I was seeing it in print. It was real. The story talked about how our parents adopted us and saved us from the war-torn country. They were, based on the tone of the article, Messiahs. So, adopting John and me was a good deed and a social statement. From that moment I could not get enough information about my adoption process, the orphanage, my birth mother, and what it would have been like had I stayed in Germany.

My snooping became more intense. I checked every shelf. I searched all bags and boxes in the closets, in the basement, in between my father's tools and in all storage bins, I rifled through all the furniture drawers, and finally, I crossed into my parents' sacrosanct bedroom; I searched their closet and chest of drawers. I carefully moved my fingers through their birth and marriage certificates, some of my father's pencil drawings, my father's and mother's Navy and Army medals from serving in World War II, and my mother's American Legion Post 404 garrison hat.

Then I found it, a worn large brown envelope containing about 30 letters from a Sister Sopatra of Monikaheim, an orphanage in Frankfurt. The letters were written on feather-light international stationery. At the other end of the same drawer was a small shoebox of photos containing orphanage pictures. After the initial discovery, I snuck into my parents' room regularly to decipher the letters and study the photos over and over again.

"Stop snooping!" cried the Old Lady.
I responded, breathless over my find, "I can't."
She murmured, "Then, it will take you a lifetime."

Despite the excitement of and jitters from finding a treasure trove, I was always careful to put everything back in the exact same order and in the exact same place.

Three

In the Revolving Door

I combed through the post-World War II black and white photos and the letters every chance I had, each time gleaning more information. Pictures eventually matched broken English words, and words eventually told a story. I sat on the floor, my back against my parents' bed, in front of my mother's open bottom dresser drawer, and I sifted through the evidence. Sometimes, I rested against the bed and just stared at the pile. The more I understood what I was reading and seeing, the more my story evolved.

During my searches, I always had all ears attuned to slamming doors or struggling keys in locks. I could hear my heartbeat. My eyes, though, were focused on the print and photos. My fingers traced the images in the photos. And my mind went wild.

Why did my birth mother give me away? Why? What did I do that was so embarrassing to her and her family?

My Shadow Family

At that time, I was one of the few villagers to be born in a hospital in a small western town of Germany. It was an uncommon event, because births took place at home with the aid of a midwife. Apparently, from birth on my life would follow routes rarely taken. It was happenstance. I found out much later that my half-brother and -sister were born at home in the 200 year-old, five-room home. The walls were two-foot thick stone and the rooms were small: the kitchen and seating area and a parlor downstairs, three small bedrooms upstairs, and no indoor plumbing. The only heat came from an oil stove in the kitchen. They lived with our mother, uncle and grandparents.

My birth parents were not married, although they lived most of their lives just two houses and a barn away from each other. My father married another woman in the mid-1950s and eventually returned to the same street. . The nature of their relationship remains almost entirely a mystery. When I finally visited Minderlittgen, no one, young or old, could give me a definite picture of the relationship between them after my birth.

The village where I was born was not far from the Luxembourg border. Before the war, the area was part of the demilitarized zone between France and Germany. The village and its farms were self-sustaining and had little material importance in the war other than to act as a buffer zone and a source of food for soldiers; eventually the American soldiers used the area as a bivouac. While the soldiers lived in the homes, the villagers were displaced to inhabit their cellars. The crops were used to feed first the soldiers. The villagers would continue to feel the effects of the war in a very personal way for years.

My birth mother and her parents were not exempt from this post-war condition, and they were relegated to their dank, stone cellar. The floor was packed earth, and a single, small chute for the potatoes, vegetables, and swines' feed afforded minimal light and air. One of my mother's brothers, a German soldier, was killed in the war, adding to their personal loss at the time. After several months, as the occupational forces pulled out of Germany, my family regained their home. A few years after that, I was born. My mother's parents were distraught about the illicit pregnancy in a village where the inhabitants were within close walking distance. They could not live with the shame. They could not live past the village talk. Being across the street from the only church, the villagers could not help but pass by my family's house and pass judgment, at least every Sunday.

After about three months in my family's home, my grand-parents forced my mother to give me away to the orphanage Monikaheim, which was more than 200 kilometers from the village.

The orphanage was operated by the Sisters of the Holy Ghost. The nuns wore the traditional long, black habits with white cinctures and large rosaries tied to their waists; only their faces and distinctively white hands were exposed. In the photos, they smiled and seemed kind. Although not pictured, Monikaheim also housed young women from the ages of 16 to 30 years old. Sister Sopatra, who was stationed at the orphanage when my adoptive mother was in the U.S. Women's Army Corp (WAC), was responsible for 17 of them. It was she who wrote so many letters to my future adoptive mother. The girls, according to her, were "very poorly on their souls and bodies." Their youth was traumatic, and the orphanage was often visited by police, either to pick up or drop them off. These young women walked in with ragged clothes, and the Sister, a seamstress, made do by making new clothes from the old fabric.

I remember nothing of the two years when I was in the children's home. I remember nothing of my experience in Germany. There is a picture of me — like a turtle that is capable of withdrawing its head and extremities and round enough to roll down the street -- barely two years old, dressed in dark, opaque stockings, and a smock dress. My hair was short, curly and red. I was sitting on a child's chair holding a horn. Standing next to me was a boy who was born a year earlier. The boy, John, held a ball. Both of us had frowns on our faces, he more than I.

Two of the black and white pictures from Monikaheim are of 13 Caucasian boys and girls between one and three years of age, and the other of 16 children between four and six years of age. In the latter picture all but one child are Caucasian; the other child, a boy, appears to be the child of a black American soldier and a white German woman. These children of mixed race were called "brown babies." Based on historical accounts, these children were ostracized and abused by the other children and caregivers. I recall an anecdote of an American military couple in Germany adopting a child who was partially African American; they found the child separate in the fetal position in a corner of an orphanage room. Knowing that the child was shunned, the couple adopted him to be a part of their family.

It is possible that many of the pictured children were occupation babies, known as "Amis," another name for Yankees and now Americans. The United States military heavily occupied Frankfurt during and after the war, but it did not prepare for the inevitable fraternization of their soldiers with local women; one night of dancing with an American soldier was followed by breakfast. The woman grew a swollen stomach, and then she went looking for "Tommy from Illinois," who had been reassigned. The military did not have enough information to track him. How does a child born in the 1950s, living in a conservative, religious country, say he or she never had a father? The German orphanages were filled with Amis, brown babies, and child victims of dead German soldiers and Jewish parents. These children are now in their late fifties and sixties. The best estimates show that between 1945 and 1956 there were more than 66,000 illegitimate children of American soldiers born in the American occupational territories in Germany.

A third black and white picture is of Saint Klaus (Germany's Santa Claus) with Georg and Heribert; they were older than four years. The two boys accompanied Sister Sopatra and my future brother to the Frankfurt airport, where John began his journey to the United States.

In all those pictures some children smiled, but a lot of them did not smile, and most of them looked lost.

"*What does it mean to be lost, Old Lady?*" *I ask, as I study the group picture of children.*

"*I'm not sure that I can explain it. When a child is separated from his parent in a crowd, and the child's eyes get bigger, as though he is about to cry, and his forehead wrinkles in fear and bewilderment, the child is lost. He isn't able to find his way.*

"*You're lost inside your heart. Sometimes you're not available emotionally to your parents. You live inside your mind of your disconnected body. I wouldn't say that you are hardened, but it's as though something external is controlling you. What do you see, child, in that photo?*"

"*I see a bunch of children lost in shame. Like me, they wonder what awful thing they did to be in this group photo. I hope their birth mothers are also lost in shame.*"

"*Do you remember reading the story of Peter Pan? There was a picture of the Children of Never Land. They were stranded, lost, and without a mother, but they were still playful, free and happy. They weren't living in disgrace.*"

"*Those children are smiling. In the Monikaheim photo only the nuns are smiling. Many of the children in the orphanage, including me, probably didn't know what was happening to them. They hope that they'll have normalcy, but unknowingly live in fear of what will happen next. Every time I do something wrong, I wonder if I'll be sent away.*"

My adoptive mother was stationed in Frankfurt from the end of the war until 1948. In a photo she was smartly dressed in her United States Army summer uniform, her twig legs sticking out of her khaki brown skirt, long-sleeved shirt and cotton tie, the garrison hat and Ike jacket. Her russet oxfords had two-inch stocky heels. She wore an oddly attractive smirk on her face. In her late 40s, Mother was an unmarried secretary, who, like many American soldiers, volunteered her Sunday afternoons at the children's home in Frankfurt. She often brought gifts to the orphans.

After returning to the United States, Mother married my father Louis. She was of Irish descent, and she wore her ancestry proudly. My adoptive father was of German descent, and he lived his origins; he followed all the traditions. On his father's side, his grandmother and grandfather immigrated to the United States from Arnsberg, Nordrhein-Westfalen in the 1830s. On his mother's side, his grandfather and grandmother migrated from Hannover. Both sides of the family immigrated with 10 children each. All families eventually inhabited the Midwest. There, Louis and his three siblings learned dialectic German in the home and school before they learned English in school. However, during World War I, some Americans and organizations became German phobic and required the schools to teach English as the mother language. In St. Louis, a city with a remarkably large German population, the citizens changed all the German-named streets to something more American; for example, Berlin Street was changed to Pershing Street, named after the World War I American hero. They also changed the name of sauerkraut to "liberty cabbage." Such was the era and place in which Mother was raised. After World War II, the sentiment grew even more anti-German. Sister Sopatra must not have been aware of the vitriolic sentiment, because she was very proud that the older children in the orphanage could already speak German; she opined that their German language would have made them more appealing adoptees.

My adoptive parents were advanced in age when they married. Louis was 45 years old, and Helen was 48. In 1951 Helen wrote a letter to Sister Alfonsa at Monikaheim:

> What I am writing about, Reverend Mother, is relative to adopting one or two children at Monikaheim. . . My husband and I can furnish very good references and can assure you that we would give a child a good home, good training, and a Catholic education.

That letter promulgated a flow of black and white photos, from which Helen and Louis chose their new children.

I was always in the "mix" to go to the United States, but my potential brothers were caught in a revolving door. As I studied the photos of the boys, I flashed back to the time I'd been caught in the Famous-Barr Department Store's revolving door. All these big adults were squashed in small, triangular sections, much like a quartered pie, pushing to exit at the right time. Everyone towered over me. I could not see when or how to exit. Mother jumped out into the store, but I was not holding her hand, and I could not shuffle fast enough. I kept looking back for my mother, and I stumbled on a big person's heels. She yelped at me, "Watch where you're going!" I was too scared to respond. I was consumed with where I was going and how to get there. Yes, I was lost in the revolving doors.

At first, Rudie Simonis was to be my brother. Later, Sister Sopatra wrote a distressful letter, stating that the orphanage just received notification from the German Youth Office that Rudie was mentally ill, and he would not be allowed to emigrate. He eventually returned to his relatives, which saddened the Sister, as though he would be mistreated by them. She ended her comment with, "— poor boy."

Weeks later Robert Maurer was the next "your own child," according to the nun. The Sister wrote in broken English:

> I was glad to read you liked the photos and I understand well
> you found the pretty little blond girl Brunhilde . . .

Whoa! My name was not Marita? A warm flush moved from my chest into my neck and my head. My cheeks felt hot.

> . . . very nice and like here to take she for your own child, in-
> deed it is a sweet child and also Robert Maurer too. He knows
> already the German language I think, this is already good. He
> is just like Brunhilde in a very good health perfectly normal.

Sister Sopatra had hoped that Robert was suitable, because if he were not, no other boys were available at that time, due to immigration restrictions. She added in her November letter:

> . . . Robert Maurer is 4 years old you can see on his picture.
> The boy is very clever, alert, smart, you will see this. You can
> choose what you prefer to do.

Something happened with Robert, though, and he was caught in the revolving door and did not make the voyage across the Atlantic Ocean.

John was the third selection, or as Sister Sopatra again wrote to my future mother, "he will be 'your own child.'" The next letter from Sister Sopatra to Helen is dated four months later:

> Surely you like this children both are sweet. John has really locy [curly] hair. . . . We hope John will be finished in June to travel to you.

A month later she writes, ". . . You can have the sweet boy John." John, born in another part of Germany, was an Ami, the byproduct of an unmarried German woman and an American soldier. His mother had been very sick and hospitalized, and was believed to be dead. John and I, just beyond infancy, played together in the orphanage, and we transitioned into brother and sister, and later friends.

I had a different background.

> Brunhilde's mother and father were very good Catholic people, but the relations did not like the child in the family, because the right husband of Mrs. Bundel . . .

But I had a different German last name—Brunhilde Komas? Was my mother married to someone else when she had me?

. . . did not return out the war, and went back to his home in *Oesterreich* [Austria], He asked his wife, Mrs. Bundel to travel over, but she did not like it. Between time, Brunhilde was born and their feel much embarrassed in their village to have this child, then also the father of Brunhilde is in this place.

My birth mother had been married to an Austrian soldier, from whom she had been separated for a few years. She eventually had an intimate relationship with someone else in the village, and I was the progeny. Sister Sopatra ends the letter with,

> Much love and kisses from your sweet children, their [they're] so happy together, John give much kisses to his sister [Brunhilde], it is quite amusing to see both playing loving one another."

I stumbled through these letters far more times than the department store's revolving door circled in a day. Some of the spellings and sentence structures were confusing. If I read the letters enough times, all the answers would come to me.

> *The Old Lady breaks my silence. "A discerning mother never forgets the child that she gives away. You are part of her shadow family--the 'what-if' family--and she is part of yours. For most people the shadow family involves more people than there are stars. Who in those stars would have been an important part of your life had different decisions been made? Look into those stars and find your mother in Germany. She's looking for you, as well."*

"*Is a shadow family something that tugs at or bullies you? And does it cause pain?*"

"*No. Your shadow family brings you comfort. It's all those people who could have been in your life. Had you a different course in life, your shadow family would have been an entirely different makeup. Not only is your birth mother there, but so is poor Rudie and Robert. If your birth mother had other children, they would also in your shadow family. As long as there are stars, these people are with you. Looking at the stars reminds you to make better, more careful choices. It makes you strong,*" the Old Lady replies, giving me a near-content, toothless smile. "*And there are more stars in the sky than grains of sand on the beaches.*"

I grow frustrated. "*If my birth mother had kept me, my adoptive parents and relatives would be part of the shadow family, right?*

"*Don't make me use big words on you,*" slurs the Old Lady. The fictional drool bothers me a little. "*I understand your sadness and alienation. Now, you try to understand the joy that a shadow family can give you. These people are obscure, but shadows are inseparable companions. They follow you around. They give you joy in that you can imagine that they are smiling at you, wishing for the moment that they will meet you. No one in your shadow family will make you feel shame.*"

"*Are you in my shadow family?*" I ask.

"*No, child, I'm only in your mind, but I'll be your companion for as long as you want. Shadows, though, are a faint reflection of who you are.*"

I would mull over what the Old Lady said throughout my life until I fully understood it.

During the war and reconstruction eras the nuns and orphanage struggled financially. On numerous occasions Sister Sopatra unabashedly asked for money to help with the children. My soon-to-be American parents sent as much money as they could. They sent coffee and money to Germany, the former being scarce, and the latter for a new sewing machine for the Sister. After John and I were claimed, my adoptive parents started paying support at the orphanage. My parents paid $22.00 a month for me. The Sister also asked that my parents buy a "basket" to carry me across the ocean. Upon completion of the orphanage's and German Youth Office's paperwork, the Americans paid Monikaheim an additional $125 for each of us children. They then paid the cost of the air flights and for special assistance flight attendants. Shortly before John and I immigrated to the United States, Sister Sopatra asked for money to buy decent travel clothes. Even after both of us were in the United States, our parents continued to send money.

Aufgeben, to abandon, give away

At three years of age, I flew from Frankfurt to Amsterdam to Montreal, then on to New York and finally to St. Louis. I was accompanied by a different order of nuns who were traveling from their motherhouse in Germany to their convent in Pennsylvania.

Later, when I was about 11 years old, I spent several "snoop times" in front of a flat map of the world. I made about as much sense of that map as I had the anatomy and physiology books. I knew the blue indicated water. I looked for Frankfurt, but I started my search in Indonesia, and moved my finger east first, then west. I could have found Frankfurt faster had I gotten on a clipper and traveled around the world. Besides starting on the wrong side of the map, my finger made little progress because I was intrigued by all the symbols and colors on the map. I did not find Frankfurt on my first try.

In my next effort, I found Germany and Frankfurt, and I memorized all the German cities that were on the map. My birth town and village were too small to earn map recognition; years later I would discover them. Amsterdam and Montreal were trickier to find because I did not know in what countries they were. Once I figured that out, I imagined straight lines between each city and embedded the picture in my head. By the time I located my entire immigration route, I knew where almost all the countries in the world were.

I met my new family at the airport, which was three miles from my new home. I wore a colorful dress, along with the traditional German gray, wool jacket with green oak leaves (from the *Eischenbaum*, oak tree, a symbol of strength) on the pockets, dark ankle-high shoes, white anklet socks, and a female version of the traditional German felt tracken hat. I carried across my chest a vinyl, red, heart-shaped purse with vinyl white piping. Blonde, curly-headed John, who had traveled to the States four months earlier, was on hand to meet me as I stepped off the plane. He was also dressed in traditional Southern German clothing. His knee breeches were *Lederhosen,* short leather pants. On his gray wool jacket's lapels were also oak leaves, like the ones I had on my jacket. He wore white ankle socks and brown Haferl shoes and a tracken hat. We could have been souvenir dolls for sale in Bavaria.

At first, after I got off the plane, John and I just stared at each other. Then, John ran up and kissed me on the cheek. The black and white picture shows us once again holding hands. I do not have any memory of this momentous reunion with John, but it must have been a joyful one. The pictures and newspaper clippings reconstructed the meeting for me. I had left the orphanage with nuns I did not know, and I was on a plane for more than 24 hours with strangers. I finally reached the end of my journey, and there to greet me in traditional German garb was my playmate. How could I know if I were in Germany, the United States or Oz? I only knew that I was reunited with my playmate from the orphanage.

Next to him were two strangers, smiling at me. I was a deer in headlights when I first met them. I had to have been baffled. I must have had frightening questions running through my little head. *Who are you? What are you saying? Why am I here? Can I go home?* They must have said, "We are your new parents." I wonder if I cried because I did not know these people, and I certainly did not know what parents were. Did I cry the entire time that I traveled across the Atlantic Ocean because I had left the familiar faces of the orphanage? Had I cried when I was first separated from my birth mother? Or did I learn not to cry? No pictures, no letters, and no news clippings revealed how I felt during these two early transitions, first from my birth mother's house to the orphanage, then to another country and another family.

I ask the Old Lady, "What's the German word for 'to give away,' 'to relinquish' or 'abandon'?"

She responds, "Aufgeben. Why?"

"I'm thinking about how often my German family has used that word since I was born, and if they are still using it." While waiting for a response, I look at the newspaper clipping that shows a black and white photo of John and me after we received our United States citizenship. The accompanying article reads:

Instead of living in a Germany still struggling to conquer the ravages of war and ever fearful of the Communist power to its direct east, Marita and John will live in the happy home made for them by their parents. . . .

The children's arrival here almost four years ago stems from the compassion of Mrs. Freimann. When she was Sgt. Helen McMark of the WAC's stationed in Frankfurt, she vowed to do her part in helping German orphan to live a decent and normal life.

"I'm sure the word was said many times when you were born. Villagers have little time but to work hard and spread gossip, and, if you're a man, drink. I can't say for sure, but I suspect hardly a day goes by that your birth mother doesn't think about you in some way."

"Is she ashamed?" Surprisingly I add, "Her bigger shame should be that she gave me away. Then I can feel like I have some worth."

"Do you want your birth mother to suffer?"

"No, but I don't want to suffer either. I live in fear that I'll get sent away again and again. I want her at least to remember me and hold my name in her heart."

The Old Lady takes a few seconds and says, "You're too young to be cautious, to worry that you will once again be sent away." I sense the start of another one of her father's fables. "A cat was very old and no longer had the energy to catch mice. The cat hatched a plan to play dead so that the mice would come to her. She hung herself by the hind legs from a peg on a door and wrapped herself with a torn pillow case. Her head and paws hung freely from the case. The mice began to scamper up the door until a wise, old mouse warned, 'Something is not right. I have never seen a bag with the cat's head at the bottom of it. Keep your distance.' The wise mouse turned to the cat and said, 'Hang there as long as you want, but I would not trust you.' So, too, you feel deceived and are now very cautious."

With that I heard my parents' car doors slam, and my warm, flushed body instantly froze. Quickly, but carefully, I replaced the letters and photos and scooted into the living room. On my way I picked up a dust rag and began work in the living room, my chore every Wednesday and Saturday, along with dust mopping the floors. My parents entered the front door and thanked me for doing my chores. What I was thinking about, though, was not the conversation that I had had with the Old Lady or why she never answered whether my birth mother was still using the word *aufgeben*. I was thinking about the rabbits in their cages that my father formerly had in the backyard. When my brother and I had first come to the United States we played with Fluffy, a fawn colored rabbit with a creamy white undercoat. For every special event, whether it was our arrival to the United States, our naturalization, or Easter, we featured rabbit as the main course. Eventually, Fluffy made it to the table, and that was the end of the rabbits. Fluffy disappeared just about the time that I became an American citizen.

Four

HOLDING THE TREMBLING RABBIT

I held two embarrassing secrets. My first secret was not originally a secret: I was adopted. My parents never kept that fact from me, and, at first, I did not keep it from my classmates. It was not until about third grade that my adoption became a burdensome secret. I don't know how this knowledge affected how I felt about my adoptive parents or treated them, but they seemed proud of their German adoptions. In retrospect, had they told me or not, I would have figured it out eventually based on the age of my parents. It was no easy feat to find out my mother's age. I never saw Mother get so angry and get her feathers up faster than when her friends and relatives broached the topic of age. Clearly she was hiding it from us children.

The second secret still haunts me.

Loving the Broken Limoges Box

People's response to learning about my adoption may be capsulized -- I was not normal.

Becky, whose large family lived in another shoe on the other side of the creek, said, "I'm sorry that you don't have a real mother and father."

Jimmy, the boy who lived behind the Barber Shop, said to me, "That must be really weird not to have normal parents."

The nun who taught second grade thought she was making me feel good by saying, "You're really special."

But as a kid I did not want to be special. I wanted to be normal. "We especially chose you" did not change that I felt freakish, although my parents never said that. The other kids were the normal children, living normal lives. After hearing these relatively condescending comments too many times, I decided to tell no one else, and my adoption became a deep, dark burden to carry. That's when I began wishing I had real parents.

"What are real parents?" interjects the Old Lady.

"Parents who gave birth to me," I lob back.

"Your birth mother and father are real parents? What have they done for you?"

"They didn't have a chance to be real parents to me."

"They gave you up, remember?"

I gape at the Old Lady as she speaks. Her nose looks particularly bulbous and worn. The woman with all the questions and all the answers.

Finally, I say, "The children with real parents live with them and have a better life. They're loved. I don't remember my mother ever telling me that they were glad that I was in their lives. My father, maybe."

"Oh, honey, you have no idea." The Old Lady lectures me with a metaphor. "My husband bought from an old man, whose wife had just died, an antique Limoges box for my vanity dresser. It was a treasured trinket with gold rose feet and muted pastel roses on the white porcelain. For me, it was priceless. One day a chicken got into the house, and the cat chased it until the bird flew out — after they had caused chaos in the house. They raced across my dresser and bumped the box, and it fell onto the floor. It cracked into three pieces. My husband repaired it, and I could hardly see the cracks. I loved the perfect box before the accident, and I loved the box after it was repaired, but it was not the same. When a child is born, there exists a perfect Limoges box, a bond between mother and child. When the child is abandoned, the box is broken. When the pieces are glued together, no matter how perfectly, the original bond is gone. In appearance, the fragile box is whole again, but in reality, the glue that binds the pieces is in the way of that once perfect bond. A relationship exists between the adopted child and adoptive parents, but it is not the same relationship that only a birth mother and daughter can experience. The relationship is different, no matter how exact the repair."

"Soooo, you're saying that my adoptive parents will never be real parents?" I feel only despair. "Once that box is broken, it is worthless."

In disgust, the Old Lady says, "You're only hearing what you want to hear. I am saying that there can be warmth between you and your adoptive parents, but it won't be the same warmth from a birth mother. Nonetheless, the relationship between you and your adoptive parents can be satisfying and cherished."

This early time marked the beginning of my rejecting my adoptive parents' love. Not knowing how else to measure love, I began to equate it with material things. It was not until much later, as a young adult, that I learned that so many of those "perfect" children with "perfect" lives had very real problems with their "real" parents. I still wonder what I could have had with my adoptive parents, had I known what do to make things better.

Hidden Tears

My second, crushing secret was that I wet the bed until I was almost 14. My parents went to the family doctor for help and learned that there are several reasons why children wet the bed. But there never seemed to be a medical solution. The doctor told them about an electrical device, a bedwetting alarm, to awaken me when my bladder started to release, but either it cost too much money or it was not the right solution.

I remember most the humiliation of waking up in a puddle of urine every morning. My parents had a torturous routine. Almost daily they yanked the sheets off me to see how bad the puddle was, took the sheets and hung them outside, moved the mattress in front of a large fan, and so on. I cowered as I watched them move about, not knowing whose temper would fly, if I'd be backhanded, or if I would be left with my own destructive thoughts. The stench has stayed with my senses, and today triggers bad memories. I tried to hide my bedwetting by changing the sheets and making the bed before my parents entered the room, but the stench was always there, and the yellow and brown rings multiplied on the mattress. The smell seeped into the mattress and never went away. I was ashamed, and my parents never told me not to be. My father threatened to put me in diapers.

Fortunately, classmates never asked me to spend the night at their homes. There was one time, though, in eighth grade, I spent one night at my only friend's house. Her father was the softball coach for our grade school team. Because my family was going to be at the farm for the weekend, the coach wanted to make sure I was home to play in the next game. So, he invited me to spend the night. Once in bed I fought going to sleep. I deliberately tossed left and right for as long as I could, but sleep won out. I awoke in a ring of urine. I jumped up and immediately made the bed, hoping that no one would know, but eventually the host would have seen the dried ring on either the sheet or the mattress. My friend Rosemary and her family never said anything to me, but they also never invited me again.

The other time that I was publicly shamed was when my parents sent me to Camp Mater Dei. For me, though, the fun was overshadowed by the dread of going to bed. There were two long rows of cabins with a large lawn between the rows. I was in a cabin with three other girls. One morning when I returned from break-fast, I found my mattress (with an outline of urine) outside in the middle of all the cabins, drying in the sun. My face flushed red and hot. I tried to pretend it wasn't my mattress, but as we walked into the cabin, the others saw that my mattress was missing. Even if my cabin mates didn't tell the rest of the camp, I knew everyone knew. The counselors knew, the people in the kitchen knew. Everyone. I did not talk to anyone for the rest of the week. To this day, I have saved a 1970 newspaper advertisement with a drawing of a little boy holding his hands over his ears, as other children yell in a sing-song melody, "JOHNNY WET HIS BED . . .JOHNNY WET HIS BED . . .JOHNNY WET HIS BED . . .JOHNNY . . ."

"It's not unusual for children to wet the bed until they're older, until about the age of seven, when the signals in the brain become strong enough to awaken the children to go to the toilet. It seems by 10 years old almost all children have control." The Old Lady's back must be setting against a psychology book.

"These signals are never strong enough for me, and I am no longer 10. I dream about having to go to the bathroom, and then wake up in a puddle. I can't control myself, and I always worry about the punishment. I fear going to asleep, and when I wake up in the morning in a ring of humiliation, I tremble, like a frightened rabbit."

When I started high school, my parents decided I should live with my father's mother and sisters, because the school was only a few blocks from their home. My parents must have warned them about my bedwetting, because when I first turned down the sheets to go to bed, I felt the mattress, and it crinkled from the underlying plastic. I was embarrassed that my dear grandmother and the aunts knew.

However, the day that I moved into their house was the night I stopped wetting the bed. After about a year of having a dry bed, I grew more confident that it was over; however, the social ostracism by peers and the ridicule from my parents are deeply embedded.

My inanimate companion has the last word: "Get over it. You bemoan what you don't have, and do not speak of what you have. You want what's perfect, and no one has that.

"A boy put his hands into a narrow-necked bowl to grab as many figs and filberts as he could. When he greedily seized a handful, he could not get his hand out of the bowl, and he lost everything in his hand. He cried because he wanted all the nuts, not just a reasonable amount that allowed him to also pull out his hand. A wise grandmother said, 'Grab only half of a handful, and you will succeed.' Count what you have, child, not what you don't have."

"But there's more to this story," I said, more to myself than to her.

Five

Wishing for Stone Soup

*A*fter I was shunned by my mother's family in Germany... after I left the orphanage... and after I was introduced to my new parents in the United States, (and before I had the Old Lady for my companion) I boarded at an all-girls' school while attending kindergarten. I was five years old. My brother boarded at an all-boys' school less than a couple miles from our home. I had no concept of money at the time, but when I look back, I realize that one year's tuition to send both of us to separate boarding schools was almost as much as my father's annual earnings. I also saw a chess game in the making. My mother wanted the best for my brother, and my father wanted the best for me, but the chess piece queen moves diagonally, vertically and horizontally, at times all the way to the other side of the board. The king moves only one square at a time. My mother, the queen, ruled our chess board.

My first true memories are from when I was in kindergarten. Daddy enrolled me in the private boarding school for kindergarten to become immersed in a strong education and to learn English. The Academy of the Sacred Heart, the first free school west of the Mississippi River, was not free by the time I had arrived. The buildings, constructed in the 1800s, housed the spirit of the school's founder and saint, Mother Rose Philippine Duchesne. The coziness and simplicity of the beautifully polished wood floors and the antique furniture were constant reminders of an atmosphere of caring, respect, and nurturing.

I stayed in a dormitory with older children. The next youngest child was in sixth grade. Except for the furniture in the kindergarten classroom, nothing in the old buildings was my size. Nothing was familiar, not the people, the furniture, the old pictures and statues, not the apparent wealth of the students. I was frightened by the new environment. Like in the orphanage, I found myself again living in a large room with two lines of alcoves. The beds were lined up in military fashion along the outside of the alcoves, and inside was a small privacy area with a chair and a small bureau for our folded clothes and a place to hang clothes. Some students had windows in their cubicles with windowsills that were at least two feet deep, plenty of room to sit and let one's mind wander. If the sun were too bright, they closed the tall, dark shutters. At the head of the room was a lone, larger alcove with a bed completely surrounded by starched white curtains; the dormitory mistress, who was a young Religious, slept there. Her alcove was off limits. Upstairs was another dormitory, with numerous alcoves completely covered with starched white cotton curtains, like the dormitory mistress' downstairs, but those alcoves were for the high school students and their dormitory mistress.

I cried a lot. The dormitory mistress, in her flowing black habit and white ruffled bonnet, tried to comfort me, but her warm words and embraces did not stop my tears. Tears are perfectly normal for a five-year-old leaving home for the first time, but I had left places more than once that were supposed to be my home. I had more primary authority figures during my short, young life than most children had in their first 20 years.

My tears were founded in realistic fear. I waited to leave again. I did not know what it was like to stay. I knew nothing but upheaval, and I grew afraid of attachment. I did not run and play with the day school kindergartners. I pretended to be busy doing something else, even if it meant sitting with my head down on the classroom table while everyone else lined up to go to the drinking fountain. I had nothing to say to anyone, unless someone spoke to me.

I don't remember wetting the bed while at the Academy, or anyone pointing out that I was adopted. The nuns did not publicly shame me or lecture to me about it. I don't remember feeling that my adoption story was terribly unique, either. All the children seemed to have a story to tell about their fathers and mothers living in other states, or a divorced or widowed father who did not know what to do with the children because he worked too much to take care of them. A couple of the children had behavioral concerns, although I don't recall noticing them. I knew from the older kids not to associate with certain girls. In general, I still was too young to do more than absorb.

On winter days it was dark outside and cold inside. About an hour before it was time to arise we would hear the pipes contract with booms and cracking as the hot water heated and rushed to the radiators and community bathrooms. At 6:30 the dormitory mistress rang an unwelcome hand bell to awaken us for early Mass. She walked up the long aisle and back, ding, ding, ding, ding . . . ding, ding, ding, ding. We jumped into our cold alcoves to get into our robes and slippers, and walked sleepily to the bathroom to brush our teeth and wash our faces. Back in the alcoves we changed into our uniforms --- a blue-gray smocked dress just for me because of my age bracket -- brushed our hair, donned our long, white veils that were secured to our heads by a sewn-in comb, and walked quietly down the hallowed halls to the chapel.

The nuns were chanting Matins as part of their morning Office. We tiptoed into the chapel and took our place in the center pews. We did not dare to sit down, only kneel. The nuns were along the sides of the chapel. Their sections were designed to sit facing center. When they knelt, they bent over and moved their small portable pre dieus, or kneelers, to face the main altar. The Gregorian chant went from the left side to the right, back to the left, and sometimes they sang. After Mass, we went into the bowels of the old building to have breakfast. We sat at big square tables, large enough to seat at least eight people. If I hadn't had a booster seat, I couldn't have seen over the table top. Later, after discovering the adoption letters and black and white photos, I wondered if that was how I had lived at the orphanage.

The Religious of the Sacred Heart were a gentle, caring group of then semi-cloistered nuns. Mother Alvena, the Mistress General of the school, often invited me into her office, which was six steps up into a large closet. She spoke kindly and softly, gave me treats, and called me (and everyone else) "Little Lambkin." During Lent, the kindergarten children stuffed little cotton lambs for Easter. They were placed in an Easter setting in an alcove that once was the back porch of the 1828 building. Mother Alvena reminded me that all children are lambs of God.

Of course, Lent introduced spring. The Academy was surrounded by prized land, the nuns' sacred cemetery, the Academy's grotto of the Blessed Mother, and the new but un-finished Philippine Duchesne Shrine. The maintenance men kept the grass cut, but the dandelions managed to escape the mower's blade, and the violets interspersed among the dande-lions were bouquets yearning to be picked. The kindergarten teacher convinced the class, without much cajoling, to go out-side and pick the beautiful "flowers" and place them before the Blessed Mother in the grotto. Like goat kids, my classmates gamboled in the fields of yellow and purple, flitting from one friend to another, crouching in twos and threes, picking the flowers while talking secret things. I crouched apart and set myself to the task.

The Religious never allowed us to go into the daffodil and tulip gardens, although they would have been easier to pick. They grimaced when we accidently presented them with a bouquet of daffodils and were gracious when presented with a handful of violets and dandelions. I raced to pick the most and present the biggest. I kept returning to different nuns with these bouquets, hoping to hear, "It is so beautiful!" "Child, you are working so hard." "I've never received such a lovely collection of flowers." I curtseyed, with a "Thank you, Mother [a salutation similar to Sister]," and walked away, making sure the back of my little dress was flattened and not drawn up. I beamed inside because I felt important and needed.

The kindergarten teacher was a gruff lay person. The class was afraid of her, but then, we were barely three feet tall and eight inches wide, and she seemed more than six feet tall and three feet wide. She always made us take naps, even if we were not tired. She stood over us glaring until we fell asleep – it was not helpful. One of my classmates surmised that the reason that the teacher wanted us to sleep was because she was the one that really wanted a nap. She not only napped, but also snored.

Every Friday night my father picked me up at the Academy, and every Sunday night I returned. The weekends were a blur, unlike the week at the Academy. Despite the tranquil memories, I hated being at school. I must have looked forward to going home for the weekends.

After the first year my father could not afford the Academy. My parents modified my brother's status from boarder to day student, and Mother went back to work to pay for my brother's private education. This time the queen moved vertically across the board, and the king retreated only one block. I started first grade at the local parochial grade school. Other than my father, brother and poor Freddie, boys were a novelty, and, so, transferring to a parochial school was a curious change.

No Claim or Right

Most of the books that I had in the first through third grades I had already used in kindergarten. The Academy taught me not only the English language, but also advanced reading. In third grade I received as an award for reading excellence, a white five-inch tall, plastic Blessed Mother statue that glowed in the dark. She was encased in a white plastic pillar grotto with a deep blue background. Academically I surpassed the average classmates, and the principal suggested that I skip fourth grade. (Grade acceleration was common in the 1950s.)

I skipped a grade, but I was not socially torpedoed by this move because I really did not feel comfortable with either group of classmates. I still pretended to be busy reading a school book when class leaders were picking teams and did not pick me. I still lied to my parochial school classmates that I had a lot to do after school with kids from the public schools.

Unlike the Religious of the Sacred Heart, the sisters in the co-educational parochial school showed signs of human frailty. In second grade, my teacher, who was searching for something in the classroom closet, was upset with me because someone came to classroom front door and asked where the Sister was, and I pointed to the back closet. I did not know what I had done wrong, but later the nun came to me and growled that she could have killed me for telling this person where she was. I took her seriously, and held my breath until the year end, hoping that I would live to see the next grade. I was completely befuddled by my mistake. This nun said things like that to other children, too, even to those children who had real parents.

In my attempt to be like the other kids, I watched them closely. I did not want them to know that I felt different, but I didn't know how to be like them. Eventually my grade school teachers described me as aloof and reserved. I was too young to understand the words, but they sounded snooty. I did not know whether that meant I was a good girl or a bad one.

So, when the Catholic grade schools pitted the classes against each other to raise money for the missions, I saw an opportunity to be positively recognized. I stole from my parents' wallets to give to the missions. I was applauded by the nuns and my classmates, but I overdid it in second grade, when I contributed 20 dollars. Who discovered it is unknown to me, but the class nun escorted me up the stairs to the principal's office. I tried to lie myself out of the pickle, but the principal didn't buy my story. I was told not to lie, even by omission, or God would punish me. This guideline was added to the extensive list of rules I already had. Among them, the parochial school nuns and my mother told me never to stick out my tongue because God will send a fork down and pierce it. Having experience with a sharp fork going through Mother's hand, I knew it would be painful. I was, indeed, afraid of Hell.

Maybe stealing the money was the beginning of my adoptive mother's dislike for me. I'm not sure, because I seemed to disappoint her egregiously in so many ways.

In fifth and sixth grade I developed into a class clown. It brought welcome attention to me. A nun hit me on the top of the head numerous times with a 6"x 4" soft-cover yellow and black reading book because of my remarks, and my classmates laughed. In sixth grade I caught the sunlight on my watch face, and I directed the light to follow a male teacher's head while he wrote on the blackboard. The spot slipped and landed on the blackboard. He quickly turned around and pitched a perfect, "fast eraser" into my chest. The class laughed, and I was temporarily happy and felt like I belonged.

> *"Belong? A term used for property? You want your classmates to own you?" The Old Lady has spent years with her back against varying dictionaries. "You want your adoptive parents to own you? Your natural mother to own you?"*
> *I shoot back, "No, I just want to fit in, to be accepted, to be brought in. I just want an identity."*

Nonetheless, once I left the classroom to go home, I still walked alone.

As much as my brother hated the farm, it was a place that kept us together as a family. Because we had no modern conveniences, we did not have a lot to divert our attention to something other than each other. I enjoyed sitting with the family on the newly slatted battleship gray porch of the log cabin. My father, his salty body cooled after the day's work in the sun, sat on the floor of the raised porch, with one foot firmly attached to the ground and the other dangling. At night he brought out the little black transistor radio for the nightly ten o'clock news, and we listened to it together. Sometimes we talked about tomorrow's chores, or which Mass we were going to attend on Sunday, which was always followed by an argument over wearing a dress. Sometimes our only comments were about the stench of a skunk. Often we sat on the porch in silence, listening to the cooing mourning doves, the cicadas, the great horned owls, and the faint sounds of the cows and roosters on neighboring farms, and, yes, the alarming cries of coyotes. When I was in this remote place, away from suburbia and all the "haves," I did not feel the pressure of not fitting in with my classmates or of being a "have not."

For the first few years, all four of us slept in the cabin's large living room, where the large hearth was, but as John and I became older, Mother and I slept in the 1800s' addition, and my brother and father slept in the living room. We used the 1800s overnight chamber "potty" chair in the kitchen for middle-of-the-night visits. I was sometimes scared when all was quiet. I heard the many bumps in the night. Raccoons and skunks settled in, squirrels screeched, and mice ran across my blanket. Snakes slithered in the attic. It was an uneasy feeling lying in bed in the dark, knowing there was only a 180-year old hook latch and lock between me and any four- or two-legged animal. I felt more secure once I chiseled the horse blanket around my body and brought the covers up over my nose. I loved it, though, when the rain came down heavily on the cabin's tin roof. Then I felt safe. The rain kept me company.

It was two or three years later, while at the farm, when I found a way to get rid of those baggy blue-gray bloomers that I had worn for modesty under my Academy uniform. My mother decided I should wear them as shorts. Mortifying. I decided that it was time to take a stand. One early morning when I went to the outhouse to relieve myself, I slid the bloomers under my blouse and walked the more than 75 yards to the outhouse. I flung the bloomers deep into an overgrown field. How was I to know that my father intended to clear that part of the field during that weekend? On late Saturday afternoon my father walked into the cabin, and announced playfully to me and my mother: "You will never guess what I found. A possum must have dragged them into the field." From behind his back he produced the despised bloomers. "I wonder to whom these belong," as his eyes fell on me.

My mother jerked her head and eyed me. I saw only her angry face and her finger pointing menacingly at me. Her disgust was magnified when she commanded, "Marita, you put those things back on and wear them for the rest of the week."

"But they're dirty," I cried.

"You should have thought of that before you tried to hide them. Throwing away those bloomers was like throwing away money."

My father did not make a big deal about it, but I felt the scowl of my mother. She was keeping score, and I was losing. Crying, I took them from Daddy, who was glaring at Mother. The king moved one step forward. I went into the other room, took off my shorts, and replaced them with the bloomers. I pulled down the legs as far as they could go without pulling the shorts top below my waistline, hoping the bottom elastic would not ride up and make me look like a squatty, ballooned ugly duckling. When my brother saw me wearing them, he waddled like a duck. That did not bother me; John was only doing what brothers do to make their sisters miserable. I was angry, though, that my father caved in to my mother's ire. The queen slid all the way across the board to confront the king, and the king moved one step aside.

In about the fifth grade, I was beginning to feel a change. I did not like myself. I was no longer only aloof and reserved, but also angry, but I couldn't put my finger on the source of my ire.

"Why am I angry?" We glare at each other for what seemed like an eternity.

The long-silent Old Lady finally speaks, "You only talk to me when you want answers, but, go ahead, talk to me. Speaking to you takes my mind off my arthritis and my sore back. Sitting in one place is not good for the body. What were you talking about? Oh, yes, you're angry. I suspect you'll always be agitated."

"Something that makes me that way is sitting on me."

"Yes, the sumo wrestler," she replies. "I've seen a lot of angry people, many who were the victims of war and poverty. Most people got over what made them angry. Some remained victims and were bitter. You, well, you don't know what's happening to you. You seem to live in constant uncertainty with little direction and even less affection and security. When my family was going through so much uncertainty, my husband told the children that as long as we stayed and worked together, we would be fine. At our poorest point, we literally made stone soup — well, we used the bones from cows and pigs

— and although we were hungry after we were finished, we laughed about it, and we talked about how we could improve our next meal. In other words, we had each other."

There's nothing like complaining when others have it worse. Hesitantly, I say, "I'm selfish to compare my family to the really poor, and I suppose I have my parents and brother." I do not remember any time that my adoptive mother showed me physical affection or stated that she loves me. In fairness, I am not sure that she expressed love to my brother either. My father, on the other hand, tries to voice his love, but it always seems awkward. The black and white photos show no warmth, with the exception of one picture from when I had just arrived in the United States and my mother stood next to me with the broadest smile.

"In your case, anger is a cowardly emotion that hides your true emotions of sadness, self-contempt, hurt, and [pause] disentitlement. The anger [pause], the anger also comes from the inability to communicate these honest emotions."

She is slurring her speech again. I ponder if she had a stroke. I am sensitive to speech patterns because I am going to a speech therapist at school, and once when snooping while my parents were out of the house, I found a piece of paper about me that said I had d-y-s-a-r-t-h-r-i-a, which must have been the name of slurred speech. I also remember the therapist telling me that sometimes people who just had strokes speak like that. She also said that I am "so far in my head" that it is difficult to get words out. The Old Lady slurs only long enough for me to realize that while I am speaking to her, I am returning to my old speech patterns.

But my question to the Old Lady is, "What's disentitlement?"
I carefully pronounce each syllable, particularly the S's, just to
make sure I am not slurring.

"You feel that you have no claim or right to your family," she
answers as quickly as I asked. "Should I say 'families,' to include
your birth mother's family?"

I forget my original question of why I am angry.

Do Boldly

By seventh grade, I was certain that the pressure on my chest was
caused by a relentless desire to return to the Academy. Every time
I recalled my kindergarten experience, I remembered the warmth
of the black habit next to me, the arm around me, and the nuns'
soft words. I became obsessed with going to high school there.

In eighth grade, along with classmate Chris Wall, I took the
Academy's entrance test. Each day after the test, I rushed from
school to check the mail for the acceptance letter. Finally, the letter
came, but it was addressed to my parents. Both my parents were
at work, and I could not wait. I sat in the kitchen staring at the
envelope. I held it up to the light and could see only that it was a
single sheet of paper. I filled the tea kettle with water, turned on
the stove, placed the teapot on it, and proceeded to steam open the
letter. I read the first sentence of the letter, and my heart plummet-
ed. It was not an acceptance letter. It took all the remaining energy
I could muster to reseal the envelope. I was not a professional mail
thief and did not do a good job. I placed the letter in between the

other mail, went to my bedroom, lay in bed, cried, and waited for the wrath of my parents. On the next day in school, Chris Wall told the other classmates that she was accepted by the Academy.

My parents could not afford the Academy anyway. My mother was a typing clerk to pay for my brother's education, but my father's salary paid for the house and the food on the table. I was a passionate 13-year-old who was not thinking through the practical issues of daily living. I wrote a long letter to the Reverend Mother at the Academy, explaining to her why I should be accepted into the high school. I sent the letter, and did not expect a response.

On a Sunday night in the middle of the television show *Bonanza*, I picked up the ringing telephone receiver, "Hello," I said, in my official 13-year-old voice.

"Marita?" said a proper, formal female voice. She pronounced distinctly every letter in my first name. "This is Reverend Mother Curtin from the Academy of the Sacred Heart. You wrote quite a letter for someone your age. May I speak with your father?" My heart was racing. She made an appointment with my father, me and the Mistress General of the Academy. After my father told me what the conversation was about, I went into my bedroom, and paced the floor with excitement.

"Slow down!" says The Old Lady. "I've never seen you so excited."

"I've never been so excited. I feel energetic! It's the first time I feel like I have some control over my life. By writing that letter, I chose my destiny. I just had a say about what will happen to me."

"Times are different. I never considered having control over my life. I just did what my parents did, who did what their parents

did, and so on," bemoans The Old Lady. "Would you have written that letter if you were still with your birth mother in Germany?"

I do not know the answer. I am too euphoric about my new-found ability.

The Old Lady adds, "My father used to say, 'Do boldly what you do at all.' What you did by writing that letter was very bold. My brother was playing in the fields one day, and a nettle stung him in the hand. He ran home to our father and cried that he barely touched the weed; yet, it buried its prickers in his hand. My father said it was because he touched it too lightly that it stung. He told my brother that the next time he plays with a nettle, grab it tightly, and it will do no harm.

"Congratulations, child, on your boldness."

As soon as my father and I walked into the Academy and sat in the parlor, I felt at peace. The two nuns, although business-like, exuded love, caring, and kindness. They agreed to accept me conditionally into the school and allow me to work there to pay my tuition.

For the first couple of years in high school I lived with my father's 92-year-old mother and his sisters. In an even tone, my grandmother gave me only two rules to follow: "Do your home-work, and do not make me pick you up at the police department."

I was shocked. "That's it? Nothing else?"

My grandmother sat in her dark oak rocking chair with her dog next to her. With her right hand she slowly rubbed the dog's forehead. In her left hand was her favorite glass rosary. I waited until she moved her finger a notch on the rosary before she said, "You're a good girl. I trust you will do the right things."

I weighed those words over and over while I lay sleepless in bed. "I am a good girl. She trusts me. I will do the right things." My grandmother owned me because she believed in me, and I was not about to do anything to embarrass her or my aunts.

I did not mind that now I had even less privacy and more people looking over me. I slept on a single, roller bed in the same room with one of my aunts who slept on a similar bed. Sitting on a folding chair, I studied in the living room on a card table. Except when the aunts were at church, they spent their nights sitting at the dining room table, sewing, paying bills, listening to the radio, planning the garden, and reading religious magazines and newspapers. The living room was dark except for the one lamp that lighted my homework. Sometimes my grandmother sat next to me in her rocking chair. She rested her head against the back of the rocker and without saying a word watched me do my schoolwork. Most of the time, though, she rocked her chair with the dog next to her, while her hand slipped through the beads of her rosary, and her lips prayed the "Hail Mary's," "Our Father's," and "Glory Be's." No one ever raised her voice at me or made me feel unwanted, and sometimes Aunt Nettie gave me a hug. When they did not want me to hear something, they spoke to each other in dialectic German. In the mornings, I felt good walking by myself those seven blocks to school, and I returned by those same seven blocks, feeling just as good.

I loved when the church bells disturbed the quiet of my grandmother's household. In the small town of Saint Charles, five churches and the Academy rang their bells on the hour, for every service, wedding, and funeral, and especially at 12 noon for the Angelus. When I stayed at their home on a Saturday night, I was jarred awake early Sunday mornings by the explosive St. Peter's church bells, followed by those of the Lutheran church, the United Church of Christ, St. Charles Borromeo Church, and others. For some townspeople, the bells might have been noise, but the cacophony soothed me. The bells took me to another world, one that was tranquil, warm and completely safe.

Welcome Home

Warm, tranquil, and completely safe. These words best describe the opposite of how I felt most of my life. Whenever the sumo wrestler jumped on my chest and took the wind out of me, I felt cold, anxious, and afraid. I carried a deep sorrow that I never knew how to express, much less to understand. Although I talked to the nuns, I could never talk about what really bothered me, because I did not know the real issues and I could not explain the weight on my chest.

During the summer months the nuns allowed me to do things that they probably would not have allowed me to do in front of other students, such as entering parts of their sacred cloister to either polish floors or help with bookkeeping. They left open the upstairs community doors, and I heard laughter, then quiet, and more laughter. Downstairs the Religious ate their meals in quiet. Sometimes I heard someone reading to them while they ate. Later, I learned that they had a vow of silence, which most of them attributed to their not having arguments with one another and being able to treat every student the same without knowing from previous nuns the students' bad or good attributes. On a couple occasions, I stood behind the stage curtain in the gym to watch the young nuns, who pinned up their skirts, exposing their black petticoats, as they played tennis, laughed and talked.

Another summer chore was to ring the noon Angelus tower bell. As soon as the nuns heard the bell, they dropped to their knees on the hard floor and bent their heads in thoughtful prayer. The figures in long, flowing black skirts and sheer veils over their bonnets, kneeling in prayer, made me believe fleetingly in God. Such intelligent women with so much apparent faith.

The convent was, indeed, a holy place, and I loved working in the sacristies of the chapel and the shrine. The sacristies were unmarred by sound. The serenity was accentuated by calming sunlight through the stained glass windows. All the cleaning and preparation was done in complete silence behind closed doors. I, too, was serene and willing to open myself to things I could not understand. The weight on my chest temporarily slid off. Looking at the sanctuary lamp, I had moments of faith and hope.

The daily routine of the Religious of the Sacred Heart had a two-fold emphasis: their contemplative life and the students. Their soft voices, kindness and respect were remarkable. Their respect for the students was exemplified in their stern, but kind discipline and their willingness to listen. When I had a bad cold, Mother Landry came to me with a "hot toddy" (hot tea, lemon, and whiskey) and a tongue-in-cheek remark that she would get into trouble if others found out about the liquor. The next morning I was cured. Once I was a couple hours late turning in an assignment, and Mother Marheineke refused to accept my paper. Later, she came to me to read it together. She did not grade it, but she spent time discussing the assignment. As she arose to leave, she hugged me and ended with a few words of gentle reproach. I felt that I would be able to look her in the eyes and not feel like a cowering dog, and I never was going to disappoint her again.

Most Academy students were insulated from the upheaval of the late 1960s. We were aware of the Vietnam War, the drug revolution, flower power, Haight Ashbury and Woodstock, premarital sex, the beginning of the entitlement era, and the civil rights conflagrations, but it did not seem to touch our little world. On one hand, that protection kept us pure, simple, and academically oriented, but on the other hand, after we had graduated, many of us were naïve and shocked when we entered into a larger world.

Unlike in kindergarten, I never wanted to go home on the weekends. My brother was having adolescent issues that sometimes involved my covering for him. My mother was never happy to see me. My father hid in the basement, watched television, or worked nonstop on the farm. On a couple occasions, when my mother and I fought, she said to me, "I wish you would go back to Germany." This prompted my retort, "I wish I could."

On the night of graduation I went home with my parents and stretched out across my bed, feeling isolated and lost. I found myself silently rehearsing the school song:

> Where the yellow old Missouri flows its waters toward the sea/ Stands a home our hearts shall cherish through the years,/A home where sunny laughter combines most merrily /And makes a gorgeous rainbow . . . .

With those words I knew I had left "home." The song repeated itself over and over again in my head until I was interrupted.

"Welcome home, child," says The Old Lady. "It'll be nice to have you here in your old room again."

"No offense, Old Lady, but I'm not feeling 'the love.'"

"The Academy taught you to be snippy? You lie on your bed, sorrowful, wishing you were someplace else. You are home."

"Home is where I don't feel like a stranger," I reply with a quickly revised attitude.

The Old Lady seems to clutch her bag a little more tightly. "Home is about those I love — my children, my husband, and my old friends. I assumed I would never be alone as long as I have friends and family, but at my age, most of my friends and family have died. So home is now my memories, remembering those I loved and those that loved me."

"So, home doesn't have a hard-and-fast definition? It can be what each person wants it to be. In that case, for me home is a sanctuary from the outside world. When I shut the door of my home, I do not worry about not fitting in or belonging."

"I think home is a sanctuary from your mother."

Throughout my life I have looked back on the Academy education and cherished the warmth of sweet memories. I gained strong study skills and a work ethic. The school taught me leadership skills in service, accountability and balance. Eventually I chose careers that exemplify those traits. I am constantly reminded how it felt at the end of the high school day to take off that ribbon of responsibility and leadership; it was a load off my shoulders, but today I am always eager to don the "ribbon" again. (The ribbon, a symbol of leadership, is literally a slender light blue ribbon that fitted on the shoulder, across the chest, and lay freely on the other side of the uniform.) More importantly, the Academy taught me how it felt to be loved. It was during my high school years that I felt what it was like to be hugged by my Aunt Nettie and the nuns.

Six

FOR I HAVE SINNED

My Youthful Sins

A s a child, I went regularly into the small, dark confessional of the parish church. As I signed the cross, I began in a hushed voice, "In the name of the Father, Son, and Holy Ghost…bless me, Father, for I have sinned." I stared through the slatted opening that was covered with a sheer material. On the other side of the veiled aperture, I faintly made out the seated priest in black, with his head hanging down and his eyes shut to assure me that he was not looking. He said, "Confess your sins."

I tried to be truthful, but I also had to perform in front of the priest. My grade school classmates and I all knew that Father Kelly was impatient, and when one was not prepared to confess, he would get mad, and the entire church could hear him yell. So, I lied in the confessional. "I lied to my parents 10 times. I stole something two times. I talked back to my parents 12 times. I played doctor once with a friend." *That was enough*, I decided. Sometimes, though, I told the truth in the confessional, such as when I got caught stealing the $20 for the missions.

Father Kelly responded, "Say four Hail Mary's and one Our Father." Mm, I could do that. After I left the confessional box, I stayed in the church long enough to do my penance, and I left the church feeling cleansed. For the rest of the day, I was a good child.

When I was 13 years old and still in grade school, I went to confession for the last time. I decided to use the confessional for the truth and for what I thought were sins. I crossed myself and gave the preface, crunched my eyes as tight as I could, and said, "I think I wet the bed because I am a bad person."

Silence.

"Father, did you hear me? I wet the bed, and I don't like my parents. I feel like something is wrong with me."

Still nothing.

I opened my eyes and stared through the veil. Father Kelly was looking directly into my eyes. When our eyes met, he quickly said, "Your penance is to say three decades [of the rosary] of the Sorrowful Mysteries." He slammed the wood shutter to the window with a thud, and opened the one on the other side of the confessional box. I said nothing more and left the box. I must be bad, because I never before had to say so many Hail Mary's and Our Father's for penance. As I left the confessional to kneel in one of the pews to atone, I glanced at the confessional box and noticed Father Kelly pulling the box curtain aside and looking at me.

Not much later I realized my sins were a constant need for attention, a sense of inferiority, an ongoing test of my worth, and a lack of empathy. My real penance was the sumo wrestler on my chest.

At the beginning of my junior year at the Academy, Mother Tainter, the Mistress General of the high school, asked if I wanted to board there. The boarding school needed a "high blue ribbon" (a ribbon that was given to a boarder and was considered the highest leadership and responsibility). I jumped at the opportunity. It was easier than living with my grandmother and aunts, no walking to and from school in bad weather, more things to do, and I would be with people my own age. To make the move even more enticing, the headmistress gave me a semiprivate room — the best in the dorm — and a roommate I dearly loved. And I did not have to worry about wetting the bed. I agreed to continue to clean the nuns' parlors, be the receptionist early in the morning and immediately after school, be the sacristan for the chapel and the shrine, take care of the overnight visitors' meals and clean their rooms, and do anything else that the nuns asked. I was theirs 11 out of 12 months, and I fought to stay at the Academy during the twelfth month.

At the end of one day when I was just removing the ribbon from my shoulder and about to hang it on the edge of a picture frame of a Picasso print that I heard a knock. "Come in." I gave a perfunctory "Hi, Jane. . . " to the girl that was a member of a clique into which I could only dream of fitting. Her group lived on the fringe, perhaps smoking cigarettes, definitely dating, and probably "sneaking out" of the Academy when it was not allowed.

"Hi, Marita," Jane responded. That hello was more than I had ever gotten from her entire group when I greeted them in the hallways. "I have a favor to ask you. Would you mind hiding this book in your room? I don't think the nuns will check your room when they do a sweep for contraband. I'd really appreciate that." The book *Candy* was notorious and a touch sexually explicit. Today the book would be practically a children's book. I never read it, but I heard the hushed talk.

The devil and the angel played a fast game of ping pong in my head. I struggled with right and wrong, being used and wanted, being accepted and not. The devil made the winning stroke, and I took the book and shoved it into the back of my desk drawer. Shortly thereafter the nuns checked all the dormitories and private rooms for cigarettes, matches (to keep the early 1800s buildings from catching fire) and other contraband. Not long after the search, I was standing before the Mistress General. I explained that the other boarders were passing the book around, and they figured it would be safe in my drawer because I was a blue ribbon. I was truthful, short of telling her which student asked to use my drawer, but she did not ask. She then gently said to me, "Marita, I am surprised at you, but I am sure it will not happen again." She reprimanded me, and although I knew I had disappointed Mother Tainter, I didn't feel like a bad person, just a person who had a weak moment.

One of my most embarrassing cries for attention came when I was a senior. I knew the nuns walked in pairs at 9 p.m. to check that the hundreds of doors and windows of the school, shrine, and convent were locked. I do not know what precipitated my need for extra attention, but I had planned to pretend to faint in the shrine sacristy and to be found by the nuns. And so I was. The next day I did not go to class, because I was "sick." The Mistress General sent someone to my room and asked me to go to her office. I knew that if I were going to her office, instead of her coming to my dorm room, she did not believe me. Once in her office, she asked me what had happened, and I lied to her. She asked more questions, and I finally said that I did not want to talk about it. "I see," said the headmistress. "We will not talk about it anymore." But she knew.

I did other things to get attention, as well. I told a friend who was a good pianist that I could play the piano, but, of course, something melodramatic (no idea what) had happened to me, and that was why I never again played the piano. Because I did not have a boyfriend, I made one up. His name was Jim (after Jim Nabors, whose voice I admired). My imaginary Jim was in Viet Nam, and we were going to get married. Unfortunately, in my junior year, he was killed by friendly fire. The improvisation was good for sympathy from naïve teenagers. I tried to keep the lying to a minimum, because I knew I would have to remember my lies for the rest of my life. Nevertheless, I yearned for attention, and I strategically did what it took to get it.

I was a member of a class of brilliant girls. Out of 34 graduates, seven were from Central and South America and were at the school only to learn English. From the remainder, though, five became lawyers and one a judge, one an archeologist, two writers and publishers, a couple of social service directors with notable humanitarian accomplishments, a couple of directors in the medical profession, and two certified public accountants. There were the A and B tracks in Latin, Math, Science, French, and English, and I was in the B track. I earned Cs in high school, partly because I hated to study, although boarders were compelled to do that. It was not until years later, when I became an English teacher and used the style of grading of my high school teacher, that I learned the reality of having a grade of C. In a grade scale of A through F, the latter which is a failure, C was average. When a student is in a class of many smart people, the bar is higher; not all students can be exceptionally exceptional. Some must be average for that level, and some must be below average. For years I was humbled by my lack of intelligence, especially after failing the high school entrance exam, but slowly I learned to appreciate the value of study and persistence.

Sins of Omission

Much earlier than most children I learned to make my bed, fold and hang up my clothes, tie my shoes, comb my hair and get dressed, although it helped to wear a uniform in kindergarten. There was no one around to do these things for me. I suspect my independence could have been mistaken for aloofness.

After moving into my grandmother's home at the age of 13, I never again lived with my parents and brother on a full-time basis. When I was institutionalized, I felt my circumstances improve, and, yet, it solved nothing. In an attempt to find a comfortable place, my thoughts grew more muddled, and I became angry.

When away from home, I was relieved that I did not have to deal with my mother, but the sumo wrestler never went away. He became heavier and stronger. Being away from my adoptive parents just gave me more time to dig myself deeper into my self-made mire. Ironically I had more breathing room, but my regrets about how I treated my adoptive parents stole most of the air from me.

College is a growing up and socialization process for most, but I was not a traditional college student. To finance my college, I received the Spirit of St. Louis Scholarship and an assistantship at Maryville University. In addition, I worked between two and three other jobs outside the university to pay my tuition and everyday expenses. I worked as a nanny for Joe Pulitzer's grandchildren and was a tax preparer for H. and R. Block. I was also a salesperson for Famous Barr Department Store, an encyclopedia company, Fox Photo Service, and fireworks stands.

It was not until the end of my first year of college that my father tried to help me with two most obvious concerns; he offered to give me $300 toward my schooling and privacy in my bedroom at home. He suggested that we go together to the bank to deposit the money. We later had lunch in a deli. Daddy was about half the size he had been 10 years earlier when he had been a strong, stocky man. He looked old, and he slumped over the table. His clothes had never fit him, but they were even baggier now. He sat, more diminished by the size of the table. Instead of saying how pleased that we were spending time together, I said, "Why now?"

Daddy barely could hold his head up, but his eyes darted at me, and he said nothing. By now I realized how weak the king is in a game of chess, and I did not respect him.

He told me he was proud that I was in college. But his efforts were too little, too late. I had already become an enraged, resentful person. Every time my father said something to me, regardless of how conciliatory, I responded angrily. Like many teenagers, I felt as though I had already lived a lifetime and bore insufferable woes. I felt old, tired, and victimized. My actions were designed to make my sickly father suffer for allowing my past to happen to me . . . to suffer as much as I had suffered. He simply hadn't saved me from my mother's refusal to love me. Of course, he was never really culpable. In fact, he was my advocate. But he was the only one that I could lash out at, because he would sit there and take it.

The Old Lady helps me out. "Anger is just a cowardly extension of sadness. Remember? We talked about this before. You could've told your father that you were sad."

I mull over the Old Lady's remark. "It's a lot easier to be angry at my father than to tell him that I'm hurt."

"It may not be easy, but it's better to be honest with yourself and others, than to mask the real problem. Your anger only compounds the challenge, but the truth might have brought instant relief, had you been honest." I know the Old Lady is right, but being honest is far more difficult than creating a mask.

The Old Lady leads into one of her stories, "A farmer had a horse and an ass. The ass was always the beast of burden, while the horse gamboled freely. The ass was not feeling well, and asked the horse to help with the burden on the ass's back. The horse refused.

After about another mile, the ass fell down to the ground and died. The farmer, seeing this, put the entire burden on the horse, including the dead ass, to carry back to the barn. Under the weight of everything, the horse said, 'Now I am rewarded for my ill-nature. By refusing to carry my fair share of the load, I must now carry everything, including the dead weight of my poor companion.' Child, be honest with yourself; otherwise, you'll live with regrets, as well."

After I dropped off my father at home, I walked away with regret, knowing that my father did not deserve my anger. I sat in my car in the driveway and cried. I hated myself because I could not tell him that I loved him. He telephoned me a couple days later to tell me how much he enjoyed our time together and that he wanted to do it again. Shortly after that, my father became gravely ill. We never had our second outing, but I would have not changed.

"Did you tell the priest about the time you hid the bloomers?" asks the Old Lady.

"I didn't think that was a sin. I privately hated my mother for making me wear those embarrassing pantaloons, but I didn't tell anyone — until now. Was that a sin?"

"Maybe a sin of omission, the type of sin where you have a duty to do something, and you don't do it as though you're avoiding good," says the Old Lady. "Your sins of omission might be that you are supposed to love yourself, but instead, you loath yourself. You are supposed to have compassion, but instead you lack empathy."

"Wow. That is the farthest from where I am. I'm focusing on having control of my life, being independent from everything, on never being poor, never being in a position where I can't walk away."

My grandmother died unexpectedly, shortly after Daddy's undiagnosed symptoms began. I was 18 and in college. Shortly before her demise at 97 years of age, she was ambulatory and living at home. We never discussed it, but I always felt that my small, slender grandmother understood that I was "a mixed up kid." She never tried to make me in her image. Her wake was one of the last to be held in the deceased person's home. I stood outside across the street at a lamp post, watching relatives and friends going in and out of the house to pay their respects, and I prayed that a God and Heaven really exists for my dear grandmother; she had devoted herself to her religion, and it was only right that her God serve her after death.

I spent the last night of the wake with my aunts. At about 2 a.m., I looked over at Aunt Nettie's bed, and it was empty. I started in the direction of the bathroom, when I noticed in the living room, Aunt Nettie sitting in a small wicker rocker in front of my grandmother's coffin. A rosary was gliding through her hands. The silence was cut with whispers, as I heard a periodic "Hail Mary, full of grace . . . ." I watched her and heard the final "Glory be to the Father, and the Son . . ." She bunched the beads in one hand, got up from her rocking chair, leaned into the coffin, held my grandmother's hand, and quietly sobbed. I could see my grandmother's face in the coffin, and I could see my dear aunt's face. I was sad for my aunt, and sad that people must suffer the loss of someone they love. I noted that the weight on my chest was temporarily gone, as though my sadness for someone other than myself was strong enough to throw off the sumo wrestler. I soundlessly stepped back to my bedroom.

My father was withering away, getting weaker and weaker, and no medical professional could identify the cause. Mother was spending most of her time getting my father to doctors, which was more difficult for someone who did not drive. My mother and I routinely had unproductive conversations about not going to college that were always the same, verbatim. Sitting at the kitchen table, with a cigarette in hand, and her invisible scorecard in the other, my mother scowled and said, "I need you here to help me."

"But, Mother, I need to go to college," I wailed.

"You don't need to go to college. I let you go to school, but now I want you here," she said, blowing cigarette smoke over the kitchen table.

"Don't go there. I have paid for my high school and my college."

"You are ungrateful that I rescued you from Germany. You owe me. . . . I need you here. Remember, charity begins at home," crowed my mother. She paused. "I am going to call the school and tell them that you need to quit and help at home." I almost laughed that she determined the college cared, but I was preoccupied with the growing weight of the sumo wrestler.

"What would I do at home, and how long must I be grateful to you for 'rescuing' me?" I begged.

She ignored my plea. "You can drive me to appointments and take care of the house. " After my father died, she added to her argument, "I 'm cutting you out of the will." Mother had unrealistic expectations of daughters, and she transferred a portion of those expectations of mothers to me.

"How old were you when your father died?" asks the Old Lady.

"19." I graduated from college when I was 20 years old.

"How old was your mother?"

"I guess 69." I am not sure where she is going with this line of questioning.

"She needs your help," my companion says somberly. "She is older, can't drive, and she takes care of a household and a sick husband. Your mother is overwhelmed. Why is college more important than your parents?"

"That hurts." Why did I insist on going to college and not take time off to help? My brother is living several states away and not available, and my parents need someone. The Old Lady is not giving me any wiggle room. She waits for me to respond. "I don't know. I'm selfish? College gives me a sense of purpose and direction? I don't know how to switch gears? I won't be independent if I drop college to take care of her? I can't stand being around my mother? I'm not a good daughter? I just don't know." I sigh deeply. "I should owe my adoptive mother no more or less than any child born to her."

After several visits to different hospitals, no one had figured out the cause of my father's symptoms. Nerve cells seemed to waste away. When he took off his glasses, dead skin peeled off his temples and nose. My father, the Renaissance man, now had difficulty breathing and swallowing. He choked easily, drooled, and gagged; his head drooped, and his speech was slurred and hoarse. Eventually he could not walk. He sat on the worn green couch in the living room most of the day. What was once a vibrant 61-year-old man had mysteriously turned into a wasted 62-year-old.

I was too young to understand what it meant to be sick. I felt no compassion for my father. My aunts tried to make me more empathetic toward him by telling me what a hard life he had had during World War II, when the war basically closed down his boiler business, but that did not help me understand his sickness. His sickness was really only self-pity, and that he was just old and lazy.

"You need to move, get active, do something," I preached.

He wheezed, "I can't."

When I visited him in one of the local hospitals, before he was diagnosed, he was very weak. He lay shriveled up in a small hospital bed, his eyes now too big for his head. He watched me walk in and did not take his eyes off me. I didn't know what that meant. He mustered enough energy to toss his emaciated right arm out of the bed with an open hand toward me, as if he wanted me to take it. I couldn't. That image will haunt me beyond my death.

Finally, my mother, Aunt Nettie, and I drove my father to the Mayo Clinic in Rochester, Minnesota, where we learned my father's diagnosis: Amyotrophic Lateral Sclerosis (ALS), also known as Lou Gehrig's disease, a disease of the nerve cells in the brain and spinal cord that control voluntary muscle movement. My father was already in the final stages of the disease.

Those months before my father's death seemed like a funeral, once a day, all day, every day.

After the diagnosis, I consumed myself with mental hoops to define my role with my mother in the event of my father's demise. My brother was in the Air Force, and he and his wife lived far away. I had the obvious duty of caring for my mother. I spent an inordinate amount of time imagining what it would be like to be her without her husband, although I did not think that the two of them were happy together; I never saw any affection between them. They never laughed together.

When my father was hospitalized, I telephoned my mother daily regarding my father's condition. Our phone calls always ended in an argument, and I always ended on the defensive. Repeatedly she wanted me to quit school and take care of my father and her. She refused to let my brother know of my father's diagnosis, and she would not allow my brother to get a dependency deferral from the military; "He [my brother] has his own life," my mother said often. She left unsaid that my life was inconsequential.

I was torn over what was the right thing to do. I could not study. I was preoccupied at my jobs. Eventually, I lost my scholarship.

My adoptive father died three months later. It was nine months after my grandmother's death, and I was 19 years old. I was with Mother the day he died. We were standing at the foot of his bed. I heard him gurgling, and then the medical staff shooed me outside the room.

"You have my sympathy," says the Old Lady.
"I don't want your sympathy. I am drowning in regrets about my father. I never told him that I loved him." My relationship

with Daddy was complicated. I loved him in my distorted way, and I know he loved me, but I can only explain "around" that relationship, not directly to it. I am not only a conflicted teenager, but also a tormented human being who does not know how to express love or trust anyone.

"You are too hard on yourself, child. You're young and inexperienced." The Old Lady's nose seems pudgier than normal.

"There were times when I wanted my father to die ...."

The Old Lady cut me off. "It's normal after long illnesses that people wish the person would die. It is quite a burden to take care of someone for an extended period."

"No, you don't understand. I wished he would die so I could get attention." I am embarrassed.

"What did you say?" she says with obvious disbelief.

"You heard me correctly. It is my most terrible sin."

I hope the Old Lady gives me absolution, but she says instead, "You did nothing wrong, although you suffer from sins of omission." The Old Lady does not need to be confessor and juror, because both of us, without saying a word, know that my penance is to live with the image of my father's outstretched hand, and me standing within inches of his bed, unwilling to take his hand into mine.

After my father's funeral, my mother wanted to go to a restaurant, but I fought with her over what I perceived as celebrating my father's death. I did not know that it was common to have a gathering after a funeral. Mother, John and I had lunch together, but it was very quiet. Later in that day, when we were sitting at the kitchen table, I asked my mother if I could take the flowers that my boyfriend

Ron had sent to the funeral home and deliver them to the Shrine at the Academy of the Sacred Heart. She exploded, "Remember, nothing but nothing is yours now! Everything is mine."

Her voice chilled me. She ranted, "You were nothing before we brought you here [to the United States]. . . . You have never been grateful. . . . . We gave you food and shelter. . . . . We spent $800 on kindergarten, and we let you go to college. . . . ."

I got up from the kitchen table, grabbed my car keys, and drove away. This time my tears were not about me, but about my father. I realized that I never saw my mother cry over his death. After a couple miles down the main road, a policeman stopped me for speeding. I looked at him through my red, swollen eyes and told him that my father just died. The blurry blue figure tenderly advised me not to drive when I am upset, and he let me go.

In response to mother's constant threats of disinheriting me, I eventually said, "Go ahead, Mother, I don't want your money. Fritter it away, for all I care." By this time it was clearly established in my family that my mother did not like me, and I stayed away from her.

Behind the Mask

One late night, returning to the college from work at Famous Barr, I turned my car into the university's main entrance and saw three classmates puking their guts out from drinking too much.

I was envious that I was not one of them. It was not the puking that I envied, but the invitation by people my own age to hang out with them. I stopped my car to see if I could help them. They refused my offer, but thanked me for stopping. From that incident I learned how to protect myself from rejection. I became very helpful, and if I could not help, I left. I took a page from Eleanor Roosevelt's life; if I cannot be accepted for who I am, I will be accepted for what I do for others. Nonetheless, I earned a degree as fast as I could to save money and to end the pressure to socialize. Graduating meant I no longer had to worry about not fitting in with people my age. I earned my degree in three years.

During the summers of my college years, I found other places to live. I stayed at the home of a friend and her mother. Occasionally I spent a night at my parents' home. After my father died, for three months I rented a sleeping room and bathroom in the inner city, where I regularly heard gunshots and screams. I had three locks on my front door, but those locks did not keep out the darkness.

Soon after my father had died, my mother wanted me to drive her to Dover, Delaware, to visit John and his wife. I stayed at her house the night before with Ron, my boyfriend. He felt sick and spent the night on the green couch. I slept in my childhood bedroom. The next morning I dressed and went into the living room to awaken him. He playfully grabbed my leg, and my mother witnessed it.

"You whore!" Mother yelled.

She startled us. I looked around to see a thin-haired, old lady, wearing a chin brace. For a second I was speechless, but I quickly recovered, and said to Ron, "Go home." Ron jumped up from the couch and left the house.

After he had left, I tried to explain to Mother that nothing had happened, but the explanation was as useless as the chin brace that she wore every night in bed to keep her waddle from getting looser. My mother did not stop yelling. "What do you think the neighbors are thinking? How could you do this? You're junk."

How could I respond to that? I'm junk.

"Get out! Get out!"

But I couldn't get out just yet, because on that day I was driving my mother to Dover, Delaware. "So, you don't want me to drive you to Dover?" I was hoping she would cancel.

"When we come back, you will move all your stuff out!" she clarified.

This was the second time she had kicked me out of the house. Although I rarely stayed there, I might stay for overnight. Only this time, I would make sure that I never spent another night in her house. An hour later we were on the road. Both of us were seething. Not long into the trip, she hissed, "I hate you."

I wanted to say, "I hat*e you*, too *"* but I could not.

The pressure on my chest was more than an onerous weight. It was painful, and I didn't know what was happening inside of me. The sumo wrestler was playing unfairly: kicking, finger bending, punching, and jabbing my chest. I was not far from receiving the embarrassing black star, a recorded black circle that symbolized that I have lost. About an hour into our drive, I was feeling faint, but I fixated on the pain. Was I having a heart attack? No, the pain was more to the right. I pulled over, got out, and walked approximately 50 yards away from the car. I sat on the side of the highway, waiting until I stopped feeling faint. My mother sat in the car, scowling, also waiting, but not once looking at me. The pain did not go away, but I eventually returned to the car, and we drove off again.

Mother then said, "As soon as we get to John's, I want you to leave and return to St. Louis. I'll take a plane home."

I said nothing.

After that, we did not say a word to each other. The drive was at least 11 hours. I drove as fast as I could, and stopped only for gas. I didn't realize that the long, non-stop drive was hurting my mother's back, and that she would need to seek medical attention on the return. I was only 19 and she was 69 years old. As with my father, I did not understand what age did to the body. When I arrived in Delaware, I dropped her off, greeted my brother and his wife, and drove away. Before returning to my one-room inner city apartment, I drove to Washington, D.C., to spend a night with a former high school roommate.

I was in a daze during my 11-hour drive back to St. Louis. My mind was a pinball machine, taking fast hits in all directions. I tried to recall a single loving memory of my mother. While living, my father must have controlled her behavior toward me, because after his death, she exuded nothing but hatred for me. For 11 hours I asked myself over and over again, "What am I doing wrong?" "Am I really evil?"

I recalled the time when I was in high school and both my parents came to Parents' Night at the Academy. I was ashamed of them because they did not dress in nice clothes like the other parents, and because they were old. I must not have been kind to them in front of Mother Tainter, because later she told me that she I did not treat my parents very well. I speculated on whether I never gave my parents a chance to be parents, and if I were the cause of all my parental troubles. I remembered the conversation with the Old Lady, the one in which we talked about never going into my mother's camp. I reminded myself that I decided very young that I did not want to be loved by them.

I arrived after midnight at my sleeping room in the Water Tower District. Normally I made a point of being in my room before dark. I parked on the street directly in front of the building, and as I was getting out of the car, I noticed a gang of young, drunk guys about three-quarters of a block away. They were milling around. I had hoped that I could sneak up the fifty steps to the front door, but by the time I unlocked all the locks and glanced at the street, they were coming my way. I quickly got through the front door way, relocked the three locks, and left the lights off. I peeked through the side of one of the shades and noticed four guys taking the steps two at a time. Next I heard, "C'mon, honey, come out and have some fun."

First, I shuddered. Then, I froze.

"C'mon, honey! "I was thinking I should call the police, but I had no phone. I stayed still, and heard more commotion among them. Then they turned and left.

"Welcome back!" the Old Lady said.

I sighed and fell onto the bed. At that moment the pain on my right side began to ease.

"Good trip, huh?" smirked my companion. She must have not heard the racket at the door.

"I will never let anyone hurt me again," I promised. "I'll walk away first."

"And if I had a cigar I would smoke it."

"Huh? I'm not in the mood for your humor," I shoot back. I listen for the noise outside, and then I continue making promises to myself, "People will have to guess who I am."

"A mask?" asked the Old Lady. "You mentioned that one time before. What good is that?"

"It'll protect me. And by the way, I can imagine you smoking cigars. You'd have to gum it, you know. Slimy tips."

"Protect yourself, eh? Between your mind and heart is loneliness," she profoundly offered. "As a child, you had asked for a private place to hide your thoughts. Between your mind and heart is that private place."

"That's where the pressure on my chest is. Remember, the sumo wrestler? He's a powerful man in a life-time tournament, and the ring is between my mind and heart, my private place." I paused, hesitant to reveal that while others seek love, I seek to prove to others that I am worthwhile.

"I guess we all have safety nets . . . ." the Old Lady drifted off, as though she lost interest, or was thinking about smoking a cigar.

I fell asleep, but was awakened by the sound of glass breaking, and, moments later, something that sounded like a gunshot. At first it was part of a dream, but less than a minute later, I was awakened by another gunshot. Red flashing lights circled my dark room. Then I heard a knock.

"Police," the person on the other side of the door commanded. I opened the door to two police officers, who told me that someone had been shot in this neighborhood. They asked whether I had heard anything. I was in a daze from the long drive and from being awakened from a deep sleep.

I was no help, but as I was about to close my door, I saw that the windows of my car were smashed. "I just need sleep," I said aloud to myself. I fell asleep, but my body was still on the road. The tires went thrump, thrump, thrump beneath me.

After Mother returned from Delaware, I continued to help her. I drove her where she wanted to go. I offered to pay for home repairs and often did extra chores. Our relationship never changed for the better, though. On one of my visits, she said, "I wouldn't want to be seen with you." I don't know what I did in my childhood, but she could neither forget the bad, nor recall anything good about me. I was twice a disappointment. I can see clearly my performance review: "Does not work well with mothers."

I was still in college when after a couple months of silence, my mother telephoned me late in the night. She was afraid that someone was trying to break into her house, and she asked me to stay overnight with her. I agreed to stop by, but I would not spend the night. The following year, shortly before Mother's Day, I telephoned my mother to ask if she would like to do something, but she had made other arrangements. On Mother's Day, she telephoned me to say that she had changed her mind, and I could treat her to dinner.

And what did I learn in college? I learned to create barriers because I was not allowing anyone else to enter my life in order to discard me. Even with boyfriends, I maintained an arm's length.

After Ron, I dated Clyde, during my last year of college. I was drawn to him because he showered me with attention, and he was handsome and exciting. Immediately after college, I moved in with him, and he eventually became my first husband. Our relationship was my first attempt to be open. Later, when I was about 23 years old, I figured out that the challenge was not to love, but to allow myself to be loved.

Part Two

Seven

WALKING LONG ENOUGH

Walking Through a Buffet

In Lewis Carroll's *Alice's Adventure in Wonderland,* Alice meets the grinning Cheshire Cat. She is lost and asks the cat which way she is going.

"That depends a good deal on where you want to get to," the cat lazily responds.

Alice retorts, "Oh, I don't much care where — so long as I get somewhere."

The Cheshire Cat finally says, "Ohh, you're sure to do that, if you only walk long enough."

Like many uncertain college graduates, I changed my course of study from philosophy, to theology (for a millisecond), then to sociology. I also took a number of accounting and business classes. In my third and final year of college, I tallied my courses and realized

I was not going to be able to find a job, much less a career, with my aimless study. I took a few additional education courses to earn a secondary education certificate to teach English and social studies.

When I was a student at Maryville University, one of my jobs was to assist Mother Barrett, one of the first nuns in the St. Louis area willing to get her hands dirty at halfway houses for criminal offenders. My job was to be her driver, often to the inner city. The Religious of the Sacred Heart's big blue Checker had a back seat with more legroom than limousines. The only thing missing with the taxi service was a combination cap on my head. It was not unusual for her to wake me in the middle of the night to drive her to a troubled offender, whether at a bar, a jail, or the halfway house. She usually left me inside the car and commanded, "Wait here." I looked around at the dark neighborhood and saw run-down homes, broken windows, and dilapidated cars, and said agreeably, "No problem," as I rolled up the car windows and locked the doors.

But college was only the beginning of a lifetime of diversions, in which I was looking for vague definitions of wholeness, belonging, and relief from the tightness in the chest.

The Old Lady interjects, "I love buffets, but when I was younger we didn't call them buffets. The Burgermeister [mayor] hosted a time and place, and the villagers brought dishes of food. The village bakery provided the bread, and a villager-farmer contributed a pig. The owner of the local meat market usually was charged with grilling the meat, but the local stube provided the beer for the cook and his assistants while standing over the spit.

"You, my dear, have a buffet of academic credentials and work. Yet, ironically, you have no direction."

"I prefer to say my educational and professional lives are smorgasbords," I respond. "Buffets are too pedestrian! True, my academic credentials in sociology, secondary education, business administration and public administration are because I'm uncertain about my job opportunities. My careers in teaching, law enforcement and tax accounting are because I could, although teaching became my passion. Teaching high school, traditional and non-traditional college students, and traveling around the world to teach law enforcement managers and executives meet my need of instant feedback. Teaching English, history, economics, business, leadership and management, public administration, criminal justice and security management challenges me. My nearly 25 years as a Special Agent and Supervisory Special Agent, investigating federal criminal and counterintelligence violations, feeds my need for power and service. Dabbling in low-level politics allows me to influence. But, you're right. No direction. No relief."

Granted, my inclination was to help the world. In high school and college I was a warrior in the fight against the aftermath of natural disasters in the United States. Every time there was a hurricane or tornado, I jumped onto the fundraiser bandwagon to raise money and clothing for the destitute. After a couple natural disasters, I wanted to leave high school and college to attend to the needy, but I was smart enough to realize that I had neither the skills nor the money. I would have only created my own disaster and been in the way of those people who knew what they were doing. I simply wanted to be a good person and in a place where I could belong by being helpful.

My volunteer work was also eclectic. I worked with abused women, wayward girls, inner city poor, old people, and special needs students. During my second summer at the Women's Self-Help Center, I brought in the *Wall Street Journal* to read during my breaks. The full-time staff had sociology degrees, and while sitting in the break room; they talked about topics that ruffled me, such as providing more community services to people that would not help themselves and affirmative action. In one conversation, a staffer asked the others for the name of a liberal therapist; the remark amused me because I did not know that when we want to heal our psyche, we may control how we heal. Prior to that remark I believed, *one size [of psychological help] fits all.* Paris, another staff member and a recovering alcoholic, manifested welcomed cynicism; she repeated regularly, "I'm always leery of teetotalers. People, who say they're doing something free for someone else, really have selfish motives. I want to know their motives." She redeemed my opinion of idealistic social workers. At any rate, my daily reading of *The Wall Street Journal* was an indicator that I was not interested in being a sociologist.

When the summers were over and I returned to teaching high school, I volunteered nights from my home. The Self-Help Center "patched" the nighttime phone calls to the volunteers' home phones. When the abused party telephoned the help hotline, she did not know that she had been transferred to a volunteer's home. However, when a phone call awakened me at 2:00 a.m., and the person at the other end of the line was an angry, drunk male that was threatening to kill me, I could not convince myself that he would not find me and do everything that he had promised. The threats were foul, abusive, and scary, and happened many times. Full moons were busiest and scariest. Eventually, I disconnected my land line in the middle of the night. That was neither fair to the frantic women nor honest. I quit.

I switched my volunteer work to something that had instant feedback and a definitive end product. Through an inner city church program, I prepared the income tax returns of poor people. I was comfortable with crunching numbers, spouting tax codes, and discussing cold details. All my clients had refunds, thanks to the earned income credit, and it was a win-win situation.

Always Loyal, Always True

There was no rhyme or reason to my activities. I engaged in them to give myself temporary direction, much like the lesson learned in Lewis Carroll's *Alice in Wonderland*. Being industrious kept me moving, although not always forward. My tryst with Clyde was not a move forward.

Clyde, the consummate salesman and look-alike of the rock star James Darren, was eventually jobless He and a drinking buddy worked together to form a couple of not-for-profit charities. I questioned where the money was really going, but I was a relatively naïve 20–year old girl, and I did not know enough about life to ask the right legal questions. When I was 22 years old, Clyde quit the "charity business" and took a job in Detroit. To be with him, I accepted a teaching position in Dearborn. He had moved to Detroit weeks before I made the move.

"What are you thinking, girl?!" The Old lady has become my conscience. "Here's a guy that while living in St. Louis threw all your students' English papers out on the sidewalk after you confronted him about seeing another girl, and now you're willing to go to Detroit for him?"

"I don't know where to go without him."

"A little dependence there? And how are you going to make this move happen? What do you know about that city?"

"Simple. It's ugly, full of racial tension, and Clyde's there." I also have no other job prospects.

"So, you're following your heart? Mm, a first." I always get uneasy when people talk about my heart.

Before I moved to Detroit, I had planned to go to Germany to see how close I could get to where I was born. My trip was not a whimsy. If I were still in Germany I would have had a better, less complicated life, and perhaps — based on my youthful logic — I would not feel the weight that at times suffocated me. It was time to seek out my birth mother, but I did not have a lot of information concerning her whereabouts. I remembered very little of the content of the letters that had flown back and forth between Sister Sopatra and my parents. The letters were still in Mother's bottom dresser drawer. I had only the name of the nun and her current address. However, the pressing question was whether I should tell my adoptive mother that I was going to Germany. If I went without telling her, a slip of someone's tongue would hurt her. If I told her ahead of time, she still would be hurt.

I lean back in my desk chair and stare again at the Old Lady. She is still clutching her worn, jade bag, still sporting a toothless grin. The only things that ever change on her are the dawn to dusk hues of greens and browns in her face and clothing. When the sun hits her face, she looks even more ruddy and worn. With a deep exhale, I whisper, "What do you think?"

The Old Lady chimes in, as though she has been waiting for the invitation, "The adoption would never have happened." I am a little confused, but I continue to listen. "We were poor. Poor people do not adopt. Instead, they give away children. It was disgraceful, but it was a necessary evil for many women. Villagers talked behind their backs, not just during the time that the mother's belly was swollen or when the child was given away, but for the rest of the mother's life. 'See her? Has she heard from her child? How many years ago was that? 20 years ago?' And with little or no work how is this single woman feeding the child? Because I see only the poor woman's dilemma, I cannot put myself in your adoptive mother's shoes. I suppose if I took a child into my home and gave her food and a roof, I'd expect at least loyalty. If I had an adopted child, I would question my parenting more. On the one hand, I think of my precious Limoges box, but, on the other, I might second guess whether the child loves me."

"I'm not telling her that I'm looking for my birth mother. I'm just taking a trip to the area where I was born. Despite what Mother says to me, I still have concern for her."

"Do you think that it was only yesterday that I was turned into a bookend? Don't be naïve; your mother knows why you want to go to Germany."

With hesitation, I add, "I can't recall ever having a conversation with her to resolve our differences. In my late teens I tried a couple times to explain myself, but her scowl and self-righteousness never let me finish. You said, by the way, that you would expect at least loyalty. I have given that to her. In spite of our strained relationship, I would not deliberately hurt Mother . . . ."

The Old Lady interrupts me: "You're not a very approachable person. You come off as strong but reserved. Always busy working, studying, never laughing." While listening to her, my mind flits back to two incidents. As one of the college nuns was exiting the convent's automobile, she turned to me and said, "You have an air of self-importance, don't you?" At first I said nothing to her. How can I have low-esteem and value, and yet exhibit an exaggerated estimate of my own importance? I was arrogant? Pompous? I watched the nun struggle to exit from the back seat. She was old and seriously bent over from osteoporosis. When she was out of the car, I responded, "No, Mother. You're wrong." I've never said that before to an elder.

I also remember a written note from one of my freshmen classmates in the high school yearbook:

Dear Solemn Sam,
We had a lot of fun I think last year. . . . I will mind you the portry, and you be good and don't ease your temper (use control and

restrain yourself, like me). . . Please stay as sour as you are and don't ever change for the worst . . .

In my attempt to veil my low self-esteem and detachment and develop my independence, I might want to exude self-importance.

"Hey, I'm talking to you," calls the Old Lady.

"Sorry, sorry."

"Tell your mother that you want to visit Germany. Let her decide what that means. If she asks more questions, answer them honestly, but don't elaborate, unless she asks. As a child, my father told a story about a hard working villager who was felling some trees by the river to build a storage shed for the wheat that was ready to be milled. His ax accidentally fell into the river. The poor farmer bemoaned the loss of his only ax. Along came a stranger, who asked why he was upset. The stranger felt sorry for him, and dived into the water to retrieve the farmer's ax. Instead, he came up with a gold ax. The stranger asked the farmer if that was his ax, and he said no. The stranger went under again, and this time he came up with a silver ax. Again, the farmer truthfully stated that was not his. The stranger made the third dive, and this time he gave the farmer not only his ax, but also the silver and gold axes, as rewards for telling the truth. After the farmer had gone back to the village and told other farmers about the three axes, another farmer went to the river and threw his ax into it. The stranger greeted this man, as well, and when he heard that the farmer had also lost his ax, he dived into the water. He brought up a gold ax, and asked the farmer if that was his ax. The greedy farmer immediately said, 'yes.' Just as the farmer was about to grab the gold ax, the stranger yanked the ax from him, and said, 'Hold on, sir, you're lying to* *me. Not only are you not getting the gold ax, but your own ax will remain at the bottom of the river.' Just be honest; otherwise, you will walk away with less than you had."*

The Old Lady gives me an answer that I do not want to hear.

Before I started planning the details of my trip, I told Mother that I was going. She did not ask any questions, but said, "I'd like to go with you." My throat dropped to the pit of my stomach. The Old Lady did not prepare me for that response. Mother was now 71, and I was 22. I had neither the diplomacy nor the guts to say "no." I certainly could not tell her that I wanted to know whether I would have been better off had I stayed in Germany.

The trip fast became my mother's trip. We visited all the places where she had been during World War II, primarily in the Frankfurt region, about 200 kilometers from my birth place. I remember very little of our sightseeing, other than we visited every old Catholic church ever built. I walked into a historic Lutheran church and was overwhelmed by the Gothic rib-vaulted ceiling, but Mother did not stay longer than seconds, once she learned the church was not Catholic. I spent my days primarily staring at and following the passers-by, wondering if one of them was my mother or a member of her family. I watched especially the people with red hair. Once I spotted a likely subject, I studied the facial features and size, conjecturing that my mother moved to Frankfurt or even still lives. I watched the children rush to their first day of school, carrying unique brief cases on their backs and *Schultüten*, colorful paper cones filled with sweets, in their arms.

I laughed; I could have been one of those fair-skinned children not too long ago. I liked most of all the ice cream stands and *Imbiss* kiosks, then the closest type to an open-air McDonald's Restaurant, and the dark pubs. There was always time for ice cream, bratwurst and beer.

We also visited a German lady that my mother had known when she was stationed there. We went to her apartment, and my mother retold World War II stories; the Americans were the heroes, and the German people were the weak recalcitrant. I pictured the already down-and-out, war-torn residents picking up the cigarette butts that the American soldiers dropped onto the streets, in hopes of eking out the last couple of puffs; the Buchenwald tours where dead bodies were left around for days for visitors to see; the American and English occupation-forced tours of the German citizenry to witness the lamp shades made of human skin and other human atrocities; and the infamous *Fragenbogen*, the military occupant's required 148-point questionnaire of all German citizens. The denazification blamed all Germans for something in which many Germans were themselves victims. My mother proudly told stories that punished all Germans and failed to distinguish the innocent from the guilty. As true as these instances were, I was humiliated that my mother dishonored our hostess. I was also frustrated that I was so close to my birth mother's residence but could do nothing about it. I tasted the bitterness toward Mother. By the time our trip was almost finished, I found myself often running my hands fiercely through my hair in an attempt to relieve the tension. Without telling Mother why, I was hardly speaking to her.

On the return layover in Chicago — about a week before my move to Detroit — I telephoned Clyde, my boyfriend, to let him know that I had returned to the States, and he responded in a cold voice, "I have found my dream girlfriend. She's a blond-haired French Canadian. We're getting married."

"What?!" And then I paused to regain myself. "Where am I going to stay? I have a job in Detroit." If he answered me, it made no difference.

His tone was chilling and matter-of-fact. "That's life. Get over it. Move on."

After hanging up, I sat in the phone booth, confused and shaken. I began shivering, unable to process what I had just heard. I telephoned Clyde a second time. As my teeth chattered, I managed to say, "Do... do... do... you really m...m...mean what you said?"

"I do," Clyde said tersely. "I've got to go to work now." Click.

My mother and I waited for three hours at the Chicago airport for our transfer. My heart was pounding loudly, and my tight, scorched throat silently screamed. I was deserted and didn't know what to do with the new job in Detroit. I didn't have a place to stay there, and I had no job in St. Louis. After my mother and I had arrived at the St. Louis Airport, I dropped her off at her home, without getting out of the car. I had wasted my time and money on the trip to Germany, and I was at my lowest point. I felt no anger, no hatred. I just knew that if I wanted to survive, I had to keep moving. I numbly followed the script that I had laid out before the trip to Germany.

I packed the car with my clothes and drove a tearful 550 miles to Detroit. As soon as I arrived, I searched the local newspapers for an affordable furnished apartment in metropolitan Detroit. In one of the worst parts of the city, I found an efficiency apartment behind a Holiday Inn, across the highway from Wayne State University. My apartment window had two gunshot remnants that were repaired with plugs. They were from the race riots. I looked out the window and saw blue lights everywhere. When I befriended a fellow teacher at the high school, she came by the apartment and was shocked. "Marita, do you *know* where you're living?" (I always hated it when people directly addressed me with a question. I knew it could not be good.) The Holiday Inn in front of the apartment building was the site of one of the first African American riots in 1967, and there were still a lot of shootings and fires in the area. The blue lights, some of the first in the country, at the university campus were because the location was dangerous, and I was living in an area known for prostitution. After that, when my colleagues asked me where I was living, I told them that I was living in the blue-light area of the red-light area, and they immediately knew where.

I had five locks on my Detroit apartment door, and not one was overkill. People in the building were either prostitutes or drug users, with the exception of me and perhaps a handful of other impoverished tenants. At least once a week I was awakened by people on drugs screaming in the hallways. One night, I woke to the noise of someone banging on my door. It reverberated; I could see light from the hallway flash into the apartment as the intruder attempted to break down the door. I laid still, wondering if I should call the police, but after a few long seconds the person moved from my door to someone else's. To add to the excitement, at least every week a car was broken into or stolen from the apartment's parking lot. I found it odd that no crook wanted my relatively new 1972 Cutlass Oldsmobile, although I removed the internal door knobs to make it more difficult to jimmy with a coat hanger.

None of that was as disturbing as when Clyde, living with his new wife, telephoned me at 2:00 a.m., asking me if I still loved him. I was haunted by the phone call more than I was by the "crazies" trying to break into my apartment. It was not long after that telephone call that he told me the FBI was investigating him for charity fraud, and that he might be indicted. The FBI arrested him on three counts of mail fraud, and he went to prison for a minimum of three years. His wife divorced him immediately.

Mother was not in the picture while I was in Detroit. Daddy had died more than two years earlier, and my brother was still in the military and stationed in Arkansas. I don't know how she got around town without our help, but she never complained about it. I telephoned her every other week to see if she was okay. She telephoned me once, to tell me that she did not like the birthday gift I'd sent her. But, frankly, I was licking wounds and totally absorbed with Clyde's rejection. It was a time of political upheaval when President Richard Nixon and Vice-President Spiro Agnew resigned, and a time of deep despair for me. I lived with continuous thoughts of worthlessness.

"Why did you even come to this horrible place?" the Old Lady asks.

"Because I didn't know what else to do . . . because I needed a job . . . because I knew I had to keep moving . . . because . . . ."

"Because you were hoping that once you were here, your boyfriend would change his mind," the Old Lady finishes for me.

"Yes." How harsh is reality?

I brood over the real reason for moving to Detroit. I know that Clyde still cares for me. Why else would he telephone in the middle of the night? But I am also being used by him. "I live in a hell hole. I drive through more slums to get to work. I return to this pit. That's my life."

The Old Lady surely is able to see my situation. She sits on the lone windowsill that looks over my narrow efficiency, 12 feet wide and 25 feet long. The apartment is furnished with a desk, a couch/bed, a small kitchen table and chair, and one table lamp. Despite the off-white rough plaster walls, it is dark. Except for the Old Lady and her bookend husband and my clothes, nothing in the apartment belongs to me.

"Now that you know your boyfriend is going to prison instead of into your arms, do you think it's time to reverse this detour in your life?" The Old Lady is at times ruthless. "Chances are slim that you'll find answers here. You need to do something to change your situation. This place gives me the willies, and I'm just an old inanimate piece of plaster."

"Moving, heh? I keep thinking that if I just move, move, move, I'll eventually stumble upon the answers. The answer is not in finding a better apartment or staying in Detroit. Here I only

think about the pain of losing Clyde." I leave out that I was unable to afford most of the apartments in nicer areas of the city.

"How are you going to find your answers alone?"

"When I open up to people, they learn my vulnerabilities and take advantage. Clyde, for example, knows that I love him, and he has hurt me. My mother knows that I am loyal, and she preys on it. When people know me, they hurt me."

"You don't know that. You're loyal and true and only 22, child. Just another detour for you," my companion says compassionately.

"No, to have a detour, I must first have a direction."

After seven months in Detroit, I pulled the plug, and I prepared to return St. Louis, which was at least a familiar, relatively safe environment. As I was about to pull out of the parking lot for the last time, a teaching colleague, who had helped me pack the car, said, "I believe you are like still waters that run deep. I wish I would have had time to know you better." His remark was as soothing as a warm, wet cloth on a tense face. His remark was also terrifyingly accurate. I was afraid that he might get close to me.

Back in St. Louis, I roomed with a high school friend. I had no money, and I slept on the floor in the apartment, but the familiarity of the city felt better than when I had lived in Detroit. After three months, I secured another teaching position.

First Meeting with My Birth Mother

Before I left Detroit, though, I wrote Sister Sopatra, telling her that I wanted to meet my birth mother. She responded that the

German law was strict about providing adoption information. I persisted and told her how conflicted my heart has been for years and how seeing my mother once might help me find peace. She responded that she might be willing to help; after all, she was 92 years old, and she did not think the German police would put her in prison for disclosing information. I then told her about my life since high school, to let her know that I was responsible and conscientious. In March 1974 I received a fourth letter, this one from the nun's acquaintance, Bianca. She asked that I tell her specifically why I wanted to meet my mother, and what I intended to do after I had met her. It was a test.

Instead of immediately pulling out a piece of stationery to answer, I paced the tiny Detroit efficiency, but doing "laps" around the narrow room was more agitating than fruitful. It was still daylight; so, I grabbed my heavy jacket and modified version of a switchblade and ventured out in the red light area near the blue light area. Still winter the air was crisp but dry. I walked a few blocks through neglected housing and automobiles without wheels on jacks. Some of the houses looked uninhabited; windows were broken or boarded, porches caved in and rain gutters and downspouts contorted and barely hanging onto the fascia, but then I would see movement through an adjacent, unbroken window. Shattered ghettoes were not new to me; I had lived in one of St. Louis' ruined areas when I was in college. But not until I walked this Detroit neighborhood did I experience the history of a once great automobile and blue-collar capital, lasting from the 1920s through the 1950s and becoming a city more known for its race riots and blighted ghettoes.

Eventually, I made my way to a bare-bones coffee shop on Grand Boulevard, across from the imposing Fisher Building. I sat in a booth with a cup of coffee and struggled with contemplating the question why I wanted to meet my mother. How do you explain to a stranger that I hope meeting my mother would alleviate the sadness in my heart and the tension in my chest? How do I tell a stranger that I hope for proverbial greener pastures?

The coffee stop did not give me answers, and I continued my walk through the campus of Wayne State University. The air was refreshing, but it did not help me develop, much less complete, my thoughts. I had two recurring ideas: What would it have been like to be Brunhilde Komas? Would I have had the same personality and characteristics? I noticed that the blue lights on the campus were more clearly illuminated; the sky was graying, and less people were on the campus pathways. I turned around and headed to the apartment before night fell. Once inside my dull studio, I sat on the couch for about another hour, and I eventually came to the conclusion that the afternoon exercise was futile.

It took me another week before I replied. I wrote, as a child I spent nights awake in bed, thinking about whether my birth mother was still alive, whether she was happy, and if she ever thought about me. Meeting her would bring peace to my otherwise unsettled heart. I meant no malice or harm to anyone, and I did not want to make any claims or force anyone else to make claims on me. I was hoping to get some stability and a sense of worth, and nothing more. Clearly my naturalized parents, not my birth mother, were the ones who buttered my proverbial bread throughout my youth. I did not tell her that I was not pleased with Mother. I remembered one of the untold but overused axioms of the Old Lady, "Do not bite the hand that feeds you." Only in this case it applied to both Sister Sopatra and my adoptive mother

In the second part of the question, what I would do after I met my mother, my answer was simple and straightforward, I only wanted to meet my mother once, get some answers, and then leave. On that part I was so sure of myself.

In the next piece of mail from Germany I received a black and white picture of my birth mother. I received the photo quickly after I had sent in my response, as though Sister Sopatra already had contact with my mother. Perhaps the photo was setting on the Sister's desk, while she awaited the correct response from me. I did not know at the time that the nun's sister had lived in a village near Minderlittgen and knew my birth mother's family. The clever old nun had all the information at her fingertips.

My first impression of the photo was that my birth mother had a sorrowful, porcelain face.

In August 1974, I flew to Germany to meet my birth mother. My emotions were running rampant, and while I could not pay attention to the details of the trip, I magically appeared at all the right places. The day before I was to meet her, I took a train to Frankfurt. I waited for some time for my transfer in the Frankfurt train station. I was entertained by the police telling transients to get up from lying down on the benches, that the waiting room was not a sleeping room. After the police left, the men fell back into the prone position. A drunken man was told to get his feet off a dining table, and instead of removing his feet, he argued with the policeman that the officer was not 100 percent German, and that he surely was Italian.

I also noticed a slight, swarthy man eyeing me as I went from place to place in the station. I left the building and roamed outside, which eventually led me to the side streets. On one of the streets, the same man that had watched me yanked me through a door that opened into an atrium garden surrounded by four walls of old apartments. He pulled me up a flight of stairs, and was trying to drag me to an apartment. I managed to pull out my five-inch switchblade and nick him. He released me immediately and ran away. I was naïve and inexperienced and did not know that some of the worst characters live around train stations.

I first met my mother in a convent attached to a local hospital in Dudweiler (a borough of Saarbruecken), which was where Sister Sopatra was assigned. I was 23 years old. The nun staged everything. I was asked to wait in a small meeting room. While waiting, my feelings were out of control. One moment I felt butterflies, another I felt nothing, and another I was angry with myself for not feeling anything. I wondered whether this whole process should have stopped with my birth mother and me exchanging photos. I was afraid of a cold meeting, because that was who I was. I also thought about my adoptive mother, whether or not I was being fair to her. I owed much to my American parents for the environment where I could succeed, and nothing to my German mother.

My mindlessness stopped when my birth mother walked into the room. She was taller than I, 52 years old, red haired, and matronly. Her eyes looked tragic, but her physique was of a woman who worked in the fields with her hands and on her knees and feet all her life. I walked up to her, gave her a warm handshake, and kissed her on the cheek. Softly and unrehearsed I said, "*Meine Mutter*, My mother," and she said, "*Meine Tochter*, my daughter." I immediately felt goose bumps on my arms. I became flush and felt drops of perspiration run from my armpits. Our eyes were fixed on one another.

At that instance, I felt no sumo wrestler, no self-loathing, and no hurt. For that moment there were only two people in my world, my mother and I. I stared at a simple, unadorned face and wondered how this person could have possibly wanted to abandon me. Whatever she did as a young person did not matter to me. What mattered was that she came to me. What mattered was that she exuded a warmth and attention that made me feel important. I was claimed and named, "My daughter."

Our visit in the convent was awkward because my German was limited to being able to find the toilets or order bread, cheese and wine in restaurants.

Our conversations were translated by Sister Sopatra. I picked up words, though. In the discussion my mother nodded to me and referred to me as "my daughter" several times. I struggled to recall a memory when my adoptive mother called me her daughter.

My mind flooded with questions, but I was afraid the que-
ries would be filtered; I did not want to irritate the nun because
she held all the proverbial playing cards of the deck. Perhaps
my mother felt the same way. My mother's first statements
were that she could not sleep at all the night before her train
trip to Dudweiler; she knew that before me—face to face--she
would be confronted with her past. Other than that, I learned
only enough to know that Minderlittgen, at the time of my
birth, was a small village, and my father lived with his wife
and five children a few houses from her. I misunderstood that
my birth father had an extramarital affair with my mother. At
the time of my birth, my mother already had two children, a
son, seven-years-old and a daughter, six-years-old. My German
grandmother was the impetus behind my being given to an
orphanage. I was an embarrassment to the family. Eventually,
through translation, my birth mother asked me not to visit the
village. Her two other children did not know about me. My
older half-brother had a family, and my half-sister had a husband and a new child. I felt comfort in sharing a secret with
my mother Mathilde.

Sister Sopatra

My brother John and I

". . . Like a turtle that is capable of withdrawing its head and extremities round enough to roll down the streets . . . and eventually he would become my brother." –Chap. 3

My adoptive mother

My childhood home

First Christmas
My adoptive parents, brother and I

John and I reunited in the United States

"German children from the orphanage are reunited here," *St. Louis Post-Dispatch*, Sept. 18, 1954 --CHAP. 3

143

My American aunts, grandmother, and father

"My aunts' hands were always busy, and their minds were always focused upward towards heaven . . . simple, gentle, little women." –Chap.8

The farm

"As much as my brother hated the farm, it was a place that kept us together."--CHAP. 5

My birth mother's home in Minderlittgen

My birth mother, 2005

My natural mother and I, and
Srs. Sopatra and Alfonsa, 1974

"My birth mother walked into the room. She was taller than I, 52 years old, red haired, and matronly. Her eyes looked sad, but her physique was of a woman who worked in the fields with her hands and on her knees and feet all her life." –CHAP. 7

My biological parents, circa 29 and 20 years old

Sister Sopatra had arranged for my mother and me to spend the night at Frau Gruenewald's house. Our hostess spoke no English; as a consequence, she and my mother spoke together, and I said nothing. When my mother poured coffee into my cup, her other hand fell to mine. She was brave to think that I would accept her contact. Conversely, when I offered a piece of cake to my mother, I felt honored to serve her. During the entire time at Frau Gruenewald's, my mother stared at me and I at her, and sometimes our eyes met. Out of politeness, I occasionally looked away. I stared at her hands, legs, feet, arms, and the natural red tones in her face. I yearned to see similarities in our features. Her eyes. Her pale skin. Her red hair.

Frau Gruenewald was a stern, but pleasant woman. She accepted no money from us for lodging and food. When I did not eat, she pointed her finger and scolded me, "Brunhilde Marita, eat!" With at least 220 pounds behind that finger in my face, what could I do but eat?

My mother and I slept in separate bedrooms. I did not fall asleep until 3 a.m. Our initial meeting played over and over again in my head. I was frustrated that I could not tell her what was in my heart. When I finally dozed off, I was in a deep, safe place. I awakened to my mother standing in the room and looking at me. She walked toward my bed and stood over me. She smiled and then sat on the edge of the bed. Hesitantly she caressed the side of my face with her hand. We again caught each other's eyes. She got up from the bed and walked out of the room. Not a word was spoken. I felt the warmth of her hand flow through my body, and I closed my eyes to capture the feeling for as long as my body would allow. It was my most tender moment.

We spent 24 hours together. My mother did not stay long because she was a cleaning lady and needed to keep her appointments. Sister Sopatra asked me to pay for my mother's trip to and from Dudweiler. (Nuns have unabashed ways of asking for money. They call on Team God.) I took a taxi with her to the train station, and walked her through the tunnel to her train. We said our good-byes, and we exchanged kisses on the cheek, but we did not budge. We stood, looking at each other in silence. I was afraid that I would never see her again. She started walking toward the track, perhaps 25 feet from me, and then returned to say, "I am at peace now." She had a single tear on her face. She turned away and boarded her train.

I returned to the hospital to thank the nuns. Sister Sopatra asked, "Are you satisfied now?"

"Yes." I had to say yes because I had written in my letter to the nun that I wanted nothing more than to see her once, but that was a lie. I wanted more.

I had no plans for the rest of my stay in Germany. I still had another nine days to travel. I also had a Eurorail train pass. I sat down in the train station to consider my next move, but my mind was filled with my mother's final words, and everything else was an intrusion. For the next couple of days, I followed my feet. Like Alice in Wonderland, it really did not matter in which direction I went, so I looked for any train that would allow me to spend the night while I gathered my thoughts.

I remembered my experience at the Frankfurt central train station and decided I would be safer waiting inside the train rather than outside. I took an empty compartment on a train go-ing to Paris. The train was not leaving for half an hour, but I felt safe, removed and within my head. Shortly after I seated myself near the window, a man came into my enclosed section and seated himself near the door. At first I paid no attention to him, but then I looked over, and he was exposing himself. I remember sighing, and then he got up and left. I permanently moved the switchblade from my daypack into my jacket pocket.

After that experience, the trip to Paris was uneventful. It was a sleepless night, but at least some place to be. I got off the train, checked the departures for Frankfurt, and boarded a bullet train that was leaving 40 minutes later. Before boarding, I stepped out-side Paris' main train station so that I could say that I had been to Paris.

By the time I reached Munich's main train station, I decided to go to Garmisch and the Bavarian Alps, although my mind was lost in reverie. Again, a man was seated in the compartment. The window was open, and once the train started moving the curtain flapped freely in my face. I was thinking how meeting my mother had been the happiest moment in my life, when without warning the man was standing next to me, graciously fixing the curtain so it would no longer beat against me. When I turned to look at him, I faced his exposed penis. He was looking down in my eyes. Fortunately, I already had my hand on an open knife. He saw the knife and quickly left the compartment. As a young woman trav-eling alone, I was a target for this kind of behavior. Months later I had a nightmare; I dreamt that hundreds of snakes were coming toward me at eye level, and as the reptiles came closer they turned into penises.

I was in turmoil, and got off at the next transfer station. My attention was see-sawing between these unpleasant sexual assaults and the happiest moments of my life with my birth mother. I was also wearing penny loafers. Two American soldiers came up to me to ask if I were an American. I asked how they had known, and they said that the penny loafers were a dead giveaway. The two men, Lynn and Dwight, were stationed at the U.S. Army installation in Ansbach. We fell into easy companionship. I don't know if it was the fact that we were young, American, or the times, but for three days we traveled together.

It was refreshing to feel protected. The two men split all the costs. Neither one was forward. They gave me the boost I needed after the contradictory emotions of the past few days. It was cathartic to go to dinner with them and over a bottle of wine to talk intelligently, or to watch them rush to ensure my comfort, or to flank me when we walked down the street.

The threesome turned into a twosome, and although Dwight was hurt, he was a gentleman about leaving Lynn and me together. Lynn offered to drive me to Minderlittgen so that I could get a glimpse of the village where my mother was living. Once there, I understood the proximity of my mother's house to the church, perhaps 25 yards, across a narrow street. We drove on Kirchstrasse and Neustrasse, which were two of the three short thoroughfares in the village. Typically, the homes were attached to the barns, and attached to other homes. I wanted to stop at my mother's house to say hello one more time, but I reminded myself that I was already dishonoring my mother's request not to visit her village.

The date to return to the United States was fast approaching, and Lynn and I were falling for each other more and more. He asked me to stay in Germany. I was torn. I likened my time with Lynn to a passionate summer in Paris, only it was in Ansbach. Meeting my mother was such a significant emotional event, that I felt I might be able to open myself just a little to someone else, despite the pain of Clyde's rejection, despite the recent experiences I had with trains, and despite my lifetime of wariness.

Still, I played it safe. I was committed to my new teaching job, commencing the day after I was scheduled to arrive in St. Louis. And I had no money. I found myself asking, what if Lynn leaves me, too? Seated on the plane, I quietly wept over the joy of meeting my mother and the loss of Lynn.

Yet, I was elated. I was alive. I was accepted.

"Are you at peace?" The Old Lady asks, as I am about to throw myself in bed for a couple hours before starting the new job. "How was the meeting with your birth mother?"

"I don't want to talk, my friend. Later," I said, as my head hit the pillow.

She lulls me to sleep with one of her stories. "It was a warm day in early spring. A boy walked by an inviting bank of a river, and could not resist jumping in for his first swim of the year. The water was deeper and colder than he had thought, and he was beginning to sink. He yelled, 'Save me! I'm drowning!' A passer-by saw the boy drowning, but instead of jumping in to help him, he gave him a lecture about how he should never swim in the river in the spring, and he threatened to notify the police. The struggling, fading boy

*interrupted him, 'Oh, Sir, please save me now, and read me the
lecture afterward!' There is a time and a place for everything.*
"Good night. Sweet dreams, child."

Walking away from Commitment

"Welcome, all, to the new school year," chirped the overly en-
thusiastic principal at the first teacher's meeting. "We have a few
new teachers to introduce." It was not until I noticed the principal and other teachers staring at me that I realized she had announced my name, not twice, but three times, that I stood up
and feigned a smile and said, "I am so glad to be here." It was my
fourth teaching job in 12 years. The first school was in a poverty
stricken area, and the officials paid me no money, only room and
board. The second school had financial issues and laid me off,
and the third was during my nightmare in Detroit. I knew the
drill. My mind was foggy. After the teachers' meeting ended, I
could not get home fast enough to my rented house to fall asleep
again, hoping that I would dream of my birth mother and Lynn.

I stayed nine years at this school, and as I had at all the
schools, I lived for my students. The profession met my needs to
be of service, and it gave me a sense of self-importance, and satisfied my need for respect, control, and most of all, approval and
instant feedback. It was a reason for existence and gave me a place
to be temporarily content.

At one o'clock on a school day, the secretary knocked on my
classroom door and interrupted the class. "I'm sorry, but it seems

to be an emergency. Your [adoptive] mother wants to talk to you."
It has been a while since I had seen or talked to her. I rushed to
the school office phone.

"Hello, Mother, is something the matter?" I asked with a
queasy feeling.

"I need you at the house to wash dishes for me," she commanded with a forcefulness that jolted me away from my efforts
in the classroom.

"Pardon me?"

"You heard me. I need you here."

Now I got it. She normally wore rubber gloves to wash the
dishes, something to do with her hands remaining dry.

"Can't you use those yellow gloves?"

"I want *you* to wash my dishes. Now." As I listened to her,
childhood memories of my overpowering mother returned. After
I finished college, I had limited contact with her, only to drive her
somewhere or do something for her. I never went to the house or
talked on the phone just to visit.

"I can't right now. I'm teaching. I'll come later this afternoon
after I finish basketball practice." I tried to talk sensibly to her, but it
was a fruitless exercise. We went back and forth. I cannot remember
if she hung up on me, or I hung up on her. About 6 p.m., I drove to
her house, but the dishes were already washed and put away.

*"Clearly your adoptive mother needs an excuse to reach out to
you, to not be ignored by you, don't you think?" says the Old Lady.*

*"I don't know. Since I've met my birth mother, I'm more sym-
pathetic toward Mother's demands. I know she's old, and she needs*

help around the house. I know that even though she says she hates me, she is trying to do the best she can."

"Maybe your mother's only means of getting your attention or controlling you is to bark orders, insisting that you be the daughter she expects you to be." The Old Lady and I often vie for the last word, although hers are more honest.

The following year, when I was 24 years old, I received a telephone call from a half-way house in St. Louis. Clyde, the man who had haunted me with that 2 a.m. telephone call in Detroit, was back in my life. He needed an exit plan (a place to live and options for work) before he could be released from prison. We established the rules that we were no longer in an intimate relationship, but that he could live in my apartment until he got back on his feet. He had lost his two children when he went to prison and could not pay child support. He had nothing, or, at least, that was my rationalization for what would become a really poor decision.

It wasn't long before we again became intimate. I married Clyde, and it was a time of pretend happiness. Unfortunately, he began to drink more and more, and he grew more violent. He worked midnight shifts, and his mornings were other people's evenings. He left work at 7 a.m. and went to the City Club, a corner bar. Like so many young women, I was hoping that I could change him and make everything better. That was not the case. He threw food at me if he did not like the taste; he hit me a couple times, and he tried to choke me. After drinking, he would demand sex, but he was unable to perform, which was, of course, my fault. When he woke up in the dark to relieve himself, he would get confused as to where he was. I often woke to find him wandering, and got up to direct him to the toilet. One very dark night I caught him about to urinate on my grandmother's 1892 antique white oak dresser, part of her bedroom wedding set. I hollered to awaken him, grabbed him and turned him around.

I decided to quit coaching basketball because Clyde said he spent his time in bars because I was never home. After telling the school administrator, I made a concerted effort to be home, but Clyde never showed up. Clyde was no longer in my life, and I had given up the basketball girls for nothing. I went back to coaching, and I also started working on my Master's in Business Administration. Shortly before our separation, I remember saying to the assistant coach, after a win, "Win a game. Lose a marriage." She had no idea what I was talking about.

While in a doughnut shop late at night, I saw one of Clyde's friends, an American Indian who continued to pride himself in wearing his native garb. He was a little scary to look at: long black, mostly greasy hair, a scar on his cheek, similar to my husband's scar, and earrings. He always wore a long knife on his side. He looked to have been around the proverbial block, and no one dared to mess with him. Sylvester and Clyde often drank together at the corner bar. This time Sylvester and I had coffee together. Sylvester was a man of few words, and for some reason that suited me.

"Where's Clyde?" he asked.

"Still working."

"Yeah?" He seemed to ponder my response a good while.

I was feeling a bit uncomfortable. "Why do you ask?"

This time he weighed his own words, while he stared at my coffee. "No, he's not."

It was my turn to consider his words and stare at him. I was considering whether I should ask the next question, or whether I would rather not know. I remembered the promise I'd made to myself when I was a child; I would never be around anyone who did not want to be around me.

"How do you know?" My eyes turned to Sylvester's dirty hands.

"He took the night off," he said as he raised the coffee cup to his ruddy lips. I pictured my husband, a stationary engineer, working in the boiler room of a local college, going from gauge to gauge, checking pressure, temperature, and other quality controls, a social man alone in a cavernous room.

"What are you saying to me?" I tend to ask questions that I really should not ask, because I am rarely prepared for the answer. It was only a couple days earlier that I had asked the basketball team members what was wrong with the team, and the girls answered honestly. Their responses were an assessment of some things that I was doing wrong. When I told them that their answers were brutal, one 16-year old player spoke up respectfully, "You should not have asked if you didn't want to know."

"He has a girlfriend at the college," he finally said.

"Why?" I again asked.

As if that were a silly question, "I don't know why he is seeing this other woman!" he exclaimed.

"No. Why are you telling me this?"

"Because you are a good woman, and he also knows it." We sat in silence until our coffee cups were empty.

"Thank you," I said as I got up and left.

A couple days after the revelation, Clyde, who had been drinking, said, "I need to get away. I'm confused about our relationship. I want go to Florida next week to straighten out my head." That was code for his wanting to take a trip with another woman.

"You don't want me to go with you?" I countered, knowing that next week was Spring Break for his young college lover.

"Nooo, I need to do this by myself." He continued, "I think I'll take my cowboy hat . . . ."

But I interrupted him, "Clyde, I know that you're seeing another woman . . . ." I could not finish because his face flashed with anger, and he grabbed my arm and twisted it behind my back. I felt a sharp pain as my shoulder separated from my upper arm. I ended my sentence with a cry, "Stop, please stop. You're hurting me!" He let go with a shove. I ran into the kitchen to get away. He approached me again as though he were going to hit me, and I quickly drew a knife from the knife block and with resolve pointed it at him. I became a wild animal, ready to take the offensive.

"I dare you to come at me," I screamed. He sobered instantly, turned, and left the house. I felt lonelier than I had when I was in college and in Detroit, and I felt trapped. I felt the blood rushing to my head, and the sumo wrestlers taking turns, pushing me off balance, twisting down, and pushing into my chest. I heard my heart beat louder and louder. Something surely was going to explode. It was time for me to leave this marriage; I was not welcome, and I became a person that I hated.

On the same day that I confronted my husband, my mother died from a massive stroke. Mother's death was overshadowed by my separation from Clyde, though. I went through the motions of the wake and funeral, knowing when to be gracious and when to be still. Clyde was not by my side. He was, instead, in Florida with his young lover. I knew people were asking in hushed tones where he was, but at that time I was not in a good place to say anything to anyone. The only clue anyone had that I was different from my aloof, almost existential façade was when I snapped at my sister-in-law when she questioned what to do with my mother's fur stole, which was left in my mother's vacant house.

The officiating priest at the funeral Mass told the audience that my adoptive mother had told him about a dream she had. He said her dream was [the much-told story] of Jesus, walking on a sandy beach next to my mother, and there were two sets of footprints. Then, there was only one set of prints. My mother had mistakenly presumed Jesus had left her, but Jesus replied that those footprints were his, and he was carrying her. I sat in the pew with my brother, embarrassed that my husband was not with me and seething that the priest had not prepared a better sermon for someone he did not know. The priest stole a religious story and lied about it being my mother's dream.

In the 30-plus years since my adoptive mother's death, I have not shed a tear for the loss of her. While relieved that I no longer fought with her, for most of those years after her death we shared a cell in my prison. She was there to haunt me, and I was there because of my sins against her. My father was there, too, but he was lying down, dead, with an outstretched arm.

Within a month of leaving Clyde, one month after my mother's death, I moved my mother's bedroom furniture into Clyde's house in exchange for my grandmother's set. Within six months I was divorced. I was 29 years old. We never spoke again until I received a telephone call from him six years later. He was dying from cancer. He wanted to make sure his final testament included a complete repayment to me. He had a different girlfriend, older and more mature. I was grateful that she was taking care of him. He finally said, "I never stopped loving you."

I did not respond, but we both gently hung up without another word.

"He has a funny way of showing that he loves you, doesn't he?" says the Old Lady. "You're hurt all the time when you are with him."

"I remember only the hurtful moments, the moments that told me I wasn't wanted. I am driven by not being where I'm not wanted. I took a chance, and that was foolish. I am learning slowly how to protect myself from that.

"The most difficult decision in my life was to divorce Clyde. I count on one hand the number of friends I have, and I am fiercely loyal to them. I was committed to my husband Clyde, regardless of how he treated me. I could not turn my back on him, and when I did, I felt like a Jekyll and Hyde. It was also the first time that I felt like a bad statistic, failing in a marriage. The dishonor of walking away from a commitment, of having to admit failure . . . ."

"Ha, who goes through something as devastating as a divorce, and thinks primarily of being a statistic? I see who you are becoming. You're withdrawing.

"You're good at self-loathing. By now you have had a lot of practice," the Old Lady says more endearingly than sarcastically. "You look at the shame of walking away from commitment, but I see that you finally did the right thing. One does not show love by beating another, no more than a master shows love to his dog by beating it."

"Your comparison could be better, but it's clear. After my divorce I volunteered at the Women's Self-Help Center. I was giving all this helpful, but fruitless advice to abused women who could or would not leave their abusers. They seemed weak and dependent, perhaps the way I was. I was grateful that I had the strength and financial wherewithal to leave, but it took a long time to muster the former. Many of those women who called the self-help center will live a hell on earth until the day they die. Eventually, I became inpatient with them, knowing they were doomed."

"So, child, where will you go next? You're always running. Detours ... and more detours. Do you have a plan, Miss Alice in Wonderland?"

"I'll continue to build a safety net," I respond resolutely.

"Also build an exit in your safety net. Hopefully one day you'll want to free yourself."

Building Safety Nets

I was not a teacher when Clyde made his final telephone call to me. He telephoned six years after we had divorced. I had moved into another profession and was living in San Francisco. It was through the FBI that Clyde had been able to find me.

My search for another profession had revolved around two predominantly male organizations: the Central Intelligence Agency (CIA) and the Federal Bureau of Investigation (FBI). I knew I wanted to continue to be service- versus profit-oriented. I also wanted the FBI job in particular because an acquaintance had told me that I would never make the grade. My response to him was, "Watch me."

I passed the Bureau's psychological test. However, the applicant coordinator, who was a crusty FBI Special Agent, apparently did not like the idea of women in the FBI, because when I went into his office for the trigger pull (a test to see how many times an applicant can pull the trigger on a 357 Magnum Smith and Wesson), he clearly stated, "You know, the only reason you're here is because you're a woman." He also made the mistake of challenging me, because I later learned that my trigger pull had equaled the average male applicant's score.

The next step was when I faced a panel of three male Special Agents. One chair in the middle of a large conference room was for me, and the men sat on a couch at the far end. They never smiled, and they never gave me an idea of how well or poorly I was doing. Prior to the meeting, I had prepared for basic interview questions, but I had always kept abreast of current events, and did not see a need for a crash course. I did, however, read a lot about the FBI and J. Edgar Hoover; so, I was primed. Low and behold, they asked how much reading I had done on the organization. I gave them a lengthy answer, and then one interviewer asked, "You said you read a couple books on J. Edgar

Hoover. Which ones and what did you find most memorable about him?" At this point the interview had already been more than an hour, and I took my chances with some levity: "I know that J. Edgar Hoover slept in the nude, and that was part of the reason no one knew he had died. Hoover did not come out of his bedroom, but no one wanted to go in to see if he was awake." The three men stoically listened and barely broke a snicker.

Most noteworthy about the interview was that one of the interviewers said that it appeared that I had low self-esteem. I was 30 years old at the time of the interview, and he was the first person to confront me with this criticism. I wiggled out of his remark by saying that it was not low self-esteem but a desire to challenge myself. If he were insightful, he did not accept that response. Most of my life was spent proving myself to other people that I was strong and good. When I boasted to colleagues that I was the best in whatever I did, I really was saying, "I hope I'm okay."

During the FBI application process, I also applied for a position as an operations manager with the CIA. Like the Bureau, the Agency was attracted to me because I was a woman with a Master's in Business Administration. Also, like the FBI, the Agency's process was long, but unlike the Bureau, it was very secretive.

I was at home on a weekend when I received a strange phone call. "Hello, Ms. Malone," a female voice said on the other end of the phone. The person did not identify herself, and rapidly followed with, "An Ozark Airlines tickets is awaiting you at the St. Louis Airport for a trip to Kansas City on the following Monday."

"Excuse me?"

"An Ozark Airlines ticket is awaiting you at the St. Louis Airport for a trip to Kansas City." She hung up before I could respond.

At first, I dismissed the call as a hoax. Later in the night I recalled having received a type-written letter on a plain piece of paper, stating that I had passed the initial test and that I will be taking a trip to Kansas City for an interview. I made a telephone call to Ozark Airlines to corroborate that the plane tickets were awaiting my pick up.

My trip to a Kansas City hotel came out a spy novel. When I went to the hotel for the interview, I had no names for whom to ask. I told the receptionist my name, and he knew immediately to send me to Room 231. I knocked on the hotel room door, and a tall, slender, white male opened it. I identified myself, and he gave me a first name, which, I am sure, was not really his first name. We sat at the hotel room's round table, but I hardly heard him because the radio was too loud. When the interview was over, he surprised me with, "I want you to meet someone else in another room." He gave me the room number, and I went directly to that room. Again, a man answered the door, and we sat down at a similar table. The interviewer spoke so quietly that I could not hear him. There must have been "rites of passage," because he then wanted me to go to a third interview room. In the last room the interviewer asked me two key questions that sunk my chances of being hired.

"Would you compromise your values to help your country?" He was really asking: "Would you have sexual intercourse with someone to get information for your country?"

"No," I responded.

"How far along are you in the FBI application process (they must have run checks with the FBI beforehand)?"

"I am moving along in the process, and I still need a medical exam." I did not know if there was a Door #4, because I sensed I had failed the interview.

I received my appointment to the FBI training academy in 1983. During training, I exhibited guts, stamina, and a level head, and my first assignment as Special Agent was to be on a bank robbery and fugitive squad. I was given a backhanded compliment when the Special Agent counselor told me that the staff must have thought highly of me, a woman, to be sent into an all-male, "macho" environment.

The Bureau transferred me to St. Louis twice, Seattle twice, San Francisco, and the FBI Academy/Headquarters. I was in and out of street Agent and supervisory responsibilities for just short of 25 years. The job opened up worlds I would have never known had I not left St. Louis. I spent time in all 50 states of the United States. I traveled the world and experienced rare cultures: the Central Asian and South East Asian people, the Caribbean and Central American people, the East Europeans, Middle Easterners, the Chinese, Russians, and Africans. I experienced the seedy side of human beings and governments, and I worked with some very dedicated people in law enforcement.

Although the entire career was fulfilling, my work life was not always filled with television-worthy excitement. For every one hour of interview or activity, I spent perhaps three hours documenting it. I often describe my job as years of boredom interspersed by moments of stark terror. Nonetheless, my career kept my mind and body occupied for long hours each day.

In December 1984, when I was a young Agent in Seattle, I paired with a male senior Agent to spend a week in a rented house next door to one of two homes that were being rented by The Order, a group of Aryan Nations men and women, known as white supremists, who had a document proclaiming war against the United States. The other Agent and I set up night vision surveillance in a couple windows to look onto the other house; we were following the whereabouts of the militants. We took turns sleeping while wearing our side arms, because if the militant group knew who we were, they would have stormed our house and killed us. Finally, at 5:00 a.m. we heard a muffled knock, and in walked a team of SWAT (Special Weapons and Tactics) members "geared up" in camouflage and heavy weaponry. Their hands, faces and necks were painted black.

Two houses were raided by five SWAT teams. It did not take long to raid the house that my partner and I were watching. The search teams gutted the house to find stolen and counterfeit money; they found money in chimneys, toilets and other less conspicuous places. In the house was a grandmotherly person, who wore symbols of the Aryan Nation. In her boots was a very sharp, long knife, and entwined in her hair was a smaller sharp object that could be used as a weapon. This slight, rough grandmother was involved in any number of robberies, to include the $3,600,000 robbery of a Brink's truck, and the murder of a Jewish radio announcer in Denver, Colorado. I was, along with another Special Agent, directed to take the woman from the house and drive her away from the two scenes so that she could not influence the other arrested individuals. For three hours the old woman sat in the front passenger seat while a gun was held to her back from the back seat.

Both houses were in the San Juan Islands, and the second house was on the beach. The leader of the militia group, Robert Jay Mathews, who also founded the Sons of Liberty, an anti-communist militia, was in the second house. Sporadic firefights broke the eerie quiet. Mathews was holding a hostage, but after a three-day hold-out with massive SWAT coverage, Mathews sent out a note with the hostage that he would not be taken alive.

Eventually, the FBI chief made a decision to throw a flare into the house and end the standoff; I was not sure of the logic, because the house was full of ammunition, and any fire source would blow up the house. Nonetheless, I was given 20 minutes to stop all sea lanes in the Puget Sound in preparation for a final solution to the stalemate. Not knowing how to stop sea lanes (and unwilling to tell the boss that I didn't know how to stop them), I contacted the Special Agent who was handling the Seattle office switchboard especially for this operation. He was experienced, and I only had to say, "Stop the sea lanes," and he took care of it. He contacted everybody necessary to complete my mission. I had to catch a helicopter ride to get on a Coast Guard cutter across the waterway, and the Agent/switchboard operator said, "I'll take care of it. You just be in all the right places." Awaiting me at the local U.S. Navy airstrip was a helicopter. I barely touched my left foot onto the helicopter skids, and the vehicle took off. I dangled for a few seconds as I struggled to get my right leg and arm into the cab. Once on the other side of Puget Sound, we landed on a hospital roof helicopter pad. Two men in white coats were waiting for me. The instant I stepped out of the helicopter, the white-coats told me to follow them down several floors of stairway out to the front of the hospital. There, with the front door open and the engine running, was a sheriff's deputy vehicle.

The deputy whisked me away to the Coast Guard cutter, which was running and ready to depart. Once the official vessel was in the heart of the Sound, the lieutenant in charge informed me that all the large ships have been advised to evacuate the Sound. The remaining vessels to warn were the small boats with no radio contact. We approached boats and delivered my instructions, and the pilots obliged. With one minute to spare, I contacted the on-scene commander to advise him that all lanes were clear.

While waiting for the next order, I watched the target house on the beach. I was in the catbird's seat. It was night, and another Agent had the responsibility of closing all air lanes; so, all one could see were the stars, the moon shimmering largely on the seaway, and an outline of a house. The commander turned off all the spotlights that were illuminating the house, and then I heard the distinctive sound of a chopper. The helicopter fired a flare into the house, and seconds later the house blew up. It was an awe-inspiring explosion with mushroom clouds, much like a nuclear explosion. The house quickly burned to the ground. I watched, knowing that Mathews was being burned to death. The young Coast Guard members, who had been giddy, became hushed.

After the smoke died down and only the fire remained, I radioed in for my orders. I was released from my duties. The lieutenant told me that he could not drop me off on the island because the coastline was too rugged for the large cutter. Instead, he radioed to the last civilian ferry of the day, which was a typical large Seattle ferry that transported hundreds of cars. The captain of the ferry advised that he had already left for the island, but he was willing to stop in the middle of the ocean for me. When the cutter and the ferry met, the lieutenant told me that I had to jump between ships. I stood on the outside of the cutter's railing, and the lieutenant instructed me that when he yelled "Jump!" I should do so without thinking. The two ships were swaying mightily starboard against starboard in the deep Sound, and I foolishly asked what would happen if I missed the ferry and fell into the water. The lieutenant advised that if I did not get crushed or drawn under by the propellers, in seven minutes I would get hyperthermia and die, but he would rescue me in six minutes. The captain of the ferry was on the deck waiting for me to jump. No sooner had I recalled how to long jump, than I heard the command, "Jump!" I successfully leapt to the ferry deck, and reactively stood up and showed the captain my FBI credentials and offered to pay my fare. He laughed and said, "I don't even want to know what is going on. I don't normally stop in the middle of an ocean to pick up a passenger."

The next day my assignment was to guard the ashes of Robert Mathews. Next to what had been the bathtub, an outline of a human being was visible . . . and a pistol. Later during that day, the experts removed the ashes without disturbing Mathews' body outline, and they flew the remains intact to the laboratory in Washington, D.C.

This story, as well as other FBI stories, gave flare to my life, but I never wanted to talk about my work or myself. When people intruded in my life by asking personal or professional questions, I clammed up, fast. One long-time boyfriend reproached me for being boring, because I would not talk about anything that would give him a clue about who I was. Other people accused me of being a conundrum; my thoughts and feelings were locked in a safe. Friends concluded that I was an excellent listener, but by listening I did not have to reveal anything. When people characterized me as "nice," I wondered if they were implying that I was either devoid of a personality or just plain boring!

"Would you be a 'nice' person, and remove this heavy book from my back?" the Old Lady asks.

"You're about as funny as a hammer toe." I do not have one, but I remember my American grandmother had a pair of them, and they had hurt her when she walked.

"Don't you wonder what my feet look like?" asks the Old Lady. "I know I do."

"What's your point, Old Lady?"

"You cannot have an open relationship without the willingness to express truthfully your feelings."

"We had this conversation before, but at a different level. I enjoy my time with other people, but I rush back to my private time. I'm content with solitude, but not content with the loneliness of my thoughts. Essentially, it's a curse not to speak

of my thoughts and feelings. When I am overcome with wonder or a revelation, I feel trapped in my body. Thomas Mann spoke about true solitaries; a solitary is not accustomed to speaking about his or her feelings, and the feelings become more intense than those feelings of an extrovert. Perhaps my thoughts are not deeper or my 'emotional experiences more intense' (Mann), but I don't know how to articulate them."

"Sometimes I see you get up from your desk and you pace," offers the Old Lady." Is that when your thoughts are more intense?"

"Yeah, I lose sight of everything except the thought. Sometimes I chew my tongue. Other times I get anxious and jump up from my chair to take a trip around the house. Sometimes I feel overwhelmed by what I have just read, and I cogitate over it. Other times I feel the sumo wrestler, clinching and taking me down with the concept. Always I share my thoughts with no one."

"You seem well suited for the FBI. You can't talk about cases, the work is important, and the job matches your dark side." She then adds, "Oh, by the way, I think it's ugly when you chew your tongue — and you make fun of my toothless mouth. Who's calling the kettle black?

"Seriously, you've successfully built multiple safety nets. You're now self-sufficient. No one can reject you without your being able to walk away from the person. Yet, you're a prisoner. Your mask and safety net confine you. You built your own prison, and you're the keeper of the keys. You might as well be a bookend."

I ignore her last remark. "It's a puzzle. I like being anywhere other than in my head, but I love my solitude. You once told me that between my mind and heart is loneliness, and that's also where I spend my time in solitude. While working cases, I my mind easily centers somewhere else.

"You also say that I've created a personal prison. My priority is taking care of and protecting me. My defensiveness is part of my safety net. As a consequence, dealings with life events become reactive. With all these protections, I am safe, but, I agree with you. I'm losing track of my soul and the essence of being, things that require a more proactive approach. Many discussions with myself in my moments of solitude are about the choice between building safety nets and finding the essence of being. Much in my life is changeable, but I needed to find first the unchanging and unchangeable nature of who I am."

"A tall order for someone who is locked up in prison. Please include in your assessment that you're cynical."

"Besides, human relationships are far more difficult to build than safety nets. Instead, I might concentrate on protecting my reputation, being a hard-working, conscientious, up-front person. Shortly before I retired from the FBI, a young Agent asked me why I worked hard up to the last day on the job, and I reminded him that when all is said and done, and I am gone, FBI employees will remember me only by my reputation.

"Oh, time to go."

"What, so unfriendly?" said the Old Lady, tongue in cheek. "But first, a story from my father. A crow stole a piece of cheese and flew to the top of a tree with his steal. A fox observed the crow with the cheese in her mouth, and plotted a way to have the booty for dinner. He decided to sweet talk the bird. 'Oh, Mistress Crow,

your wings shine so bright. Your breast is a breast of an eagle. Your talons are made of steel. I have not heard your voice before, but I am sure that it surpasses any other bird, just as your beauty does.' The crow loved the flattery, especially the part about her voice. Other crows told her that her caw was weak and unattractive. She decided to caw loudly and beautifully, as never before, and the cheese dropped into the mouth of the fox. As he walked away with his dinner, he gave the following advice to the crow, 'The next time someone praises your beauty, be sure to hold your tongue.'"

"Flatterers are not to be trusted, my friend. You must have flattered me when you said I'd make a good bookend. Thanks for the 'compliment'!"

"No, I'm flattering you on how pleased you are to build these nets, while keeping out the very thing that might free you from your rootless, detached self. Try enjoying your solitude and don't invite the loneliness." *Her laugh deepens the crow's feet at the outer corners of her eyes.*

Changing Scenery

I was restless. Since college graduation, I had had 16 job changes, 10 in the FBI. After three or four years at a job, I looked for change . . . for new places to challenge me and help me to feel fulfilled. In my lifetime I moved to 27 residences. My personal trips to exotic places were for the purpose of either finding fulfillment or escape, never for mere enjoyment. Eventually, I found two ways to quell the restiveness.

When I was a young adult, my car battery died. A neighbor jump-started the battery to get me to an auto repair shop. The repairman tested the battery and confirmed that I needed a new one. "You know," he said, "when there is no energy, there is literally no energy."

"Excuse me?" I said politely, but I was thinking, *you think I'm an idiot?* This repairman must be a philosopher who could not find a job in his discipline.

Perhaps I was looking at him quizzically, which was better than what I was thinking, because he said, "Really!"

It was time to cut to the chase. "Sir, I'm not understanding what you are saying. I need a battery, right?"

"You asked whether I could just recharge the current battery, instead of buying a new one. All new batteries come charged with energy, but eventually all the energy is completely drained and not rechargeable. Your battery no longer has the energy to make energy, and it takes energy to make energy. You need a new battery." After he finished his remarks, he walked away to find an appropriate replacement, giving him plenty of time to mumble repeatedly, "women and autos . . ." "women and autos . . . ."

A few years later, it dawned on me. I could not make things happen in my search to throw off the weight on my chest, unless I moved to do something. So, I made my own energy. I became an avid runner. Running was a channel to create more energy and to clear my thoughts. It was my "restart" button; at the end of the run, my perspectives and solutions were fresh, clear and logical. After running I was energized to do something productive. I spent less time sitting and thinking about safety nets. "It takes energy to make energy." That battery was the best thing I ever bought.

The second way to quiet the restlessness was through nature. I went to nature, hoping that it would provide clarity and respite. Being in the mountains was the closest thing to my image of happiness. There was nothing more uplifting than painfully traipsing at elevations above the tree line, sitting alone at a campfire by a mountain lake with peaks of granite completely embracing me. At night, the stars battled against each other to be distinctive in the darkest of dark skies. More stars than people in the past and present. (It was overwhelming when I reflected on my shadow family at the same time.) At dusk and dawn I studied the sunrise and sunset as they captured the essence of magnificence and timelessness; only two moments were significant times, when the sun rises and the sun sets, the healing initiated by the sunset and the opportunity of a new day in the sunrise. Eventually, I learned to use every sunrise and sunset, regardless of where I was, as a personal gift to my spirit, as a reminder that each day is not the same, and the mood of the day is what I make of it. With the absence of time constraints, life was a bit clearer.

But, when I returned to the daily rush of normalcy, I found most clarity was gone, with the exception of not making time so important. Nature only "rebooted" me so that I could contend with those things that were unsettled in my heart.

And the sea . . .

"Have you ever been to the sea, my friend?" The Old Lady looks like I just awakened her.

She clears her throat. "The sea?" she says vigorously. I've never been there. Actually I've never been anywhere. Our big events were the village parades and festivals, with club bands from other villages, and, of course, lots of church events. Sunday coffee and cake sponsored by a church or a Burgermeister [mayor] were always fun." She was talking like a school girl who was caught napping in class and was trying to work around the teacher's question that she didn't completely hear.

"The sea rushes onto the beaches to wash away traces of imprints in the sand, to swallow the impressions to leave room for the new. The old becomes forgotten. When the waves rush in, I sense a fresh surge, a cleansing of the troublesome and burdensome, and when the water recedes, it takes away the weight of my thoughts, and leaves a featherweight heart." I must be talking to myself. "Are you listening to me at all?"

"Yeah, yeah, whatever happened before is gone," she says dismissively. It must be the orange lighting from the sunset that streams through the window onto her face, erasing the dark edges of her eyes and mouth. "I understand what you're saying, how nature offers you a respite. But even after your trips to nature, you eventually become edgy again.

"That reminds me of one of my father's stories. A raven was quite comfortable picking up scraps, but he became dissatisfied when he saw a swan, floating gracefully on the river. 'What makes that swan so white and beautiful?' he asked himself. He watched the swan for quite a while, and decided that the water was magic. The raven left his comfortable perch and sought out pools and streams, hoping the water would turn his black feathers as white as the swan's. He washed and plumed his feathers for a long time, but nothing changed. His plumage *remained black, and eventually, he died for lack of his usual food.*

"In your case, I don't think that a change of scenery will change who you are."

In Virginia, I lived in a rural area that was removed from the notorious Washington D.C. Beltway traffic jams. Spring was beautiful in the farmlands with fields of emerald green wheat and yellow buttercups. Worn, white Mennonite farmhouses were surrounded by tulips, expiring crocuses, and purple flocks. Many of the gray, rundown barns were starkly contrasted by the bright colors of the season. Bearded farmers wearing straw hats mended and whitewashed the wood fences while the black and white dairy cows lazily ruminated on the nearby bundles of hay. For miles I could drive by the rolling, freshly plowed fields that ran along the swollen creeks and patches of woods. The greens were as varied as a large box of crayons: celery green, pumice green, bluegrass green, and cedar green. I sometimes stumbled upon ruins from the Civil War era, or a piece of cemetery that was overgrown with blossoming vines and weeds, or daffodils in a small open area, the last being an indication of remnants of an old farmhouse. I looked above the fields to see the flocks of returning geese and birds and the haze of the distant blue Shenandoah Mountains. While I drove, I smelled the sweetness of the lilacs and the pungent barn odors.

Eventually I became more satisfied with my life, once I decided that contentment was not the fulfillment of all that I wanted, but the realization of what I already had. Signs, such as the gentle, cool wind against my face and arms, the evening noises of bullfrogs and crickets, cinematic sunrises and sunsets, and lone flowers blowing in the wind, were constant reminders that I was alive and grateful for what I had. I was content to know that if I wanted to do something else, I had the wherewithal to do it: the money, the gumption, and the attitude.

Walking Past Unanswered Letters

After visiting my birth mother in 1974, communication between us was sparse. She had written two short notes, wanting to hear from me, telling me that she finally remarried, and asking me to visit again, only this time, to her home. I questioned whether or not I should let go of her and accept that my adoptive parents were my only parents — end of story. I did not respond. However, on the first anniversary of meeting my birth mother, I wrote a long letter. Over a period of 20-plus years, I had written two long letters. The letters were informative about my work and personal life. I never shared my opinion on being adopted or being given away. I never received a response from her.

By 1998, because I had not heard from her, I presumed that she had died, but I still wrote a third letter, telling her about my five years of being cancer free after a bout in 1993, my marriage to my present husband and other changes in my life. Again, she did not respond. Still, the postal service never returned any of the letters to me. Someone must have read them.

"Why didn't you respond right away when your birth mother wrote a small note? Surely she went to the mailbox daily hoping to receive a return note from you." The Old Lady doesn't waste time getting to the point, except when she feels like telling a story.

"I couldn't decide what was appropriate. First, if I started a new relationship with my birth mother, how fair would I have been to my adoptive mother? Second, if I wrote back, would I be making my life more complicated? I am having a difficult time coping with what is, and I do not want the difficulties that come with what could be. The biggest issue, though, is our language barrier; I want to talk to her, but I do not want her to misunderstand what I am saying. I am intimidated by the language."

"Your mother took some brave steps: first, meeting you, and second, inviting you into her home and village. She knew that her secret would be told again throughout the village. And you don't respond to her notes?" asks the Old Lady. "Think of what she went through to get to the point of meeting you? Frankly, I think you're rude not to write her."

"That's why I don't need enemies. I have you as a friend." I reasoned I was doing the right thing. "Hmm, had I written back, perhaps my life would have been entirely different. Some members of my shadow family were created when I chose not to respond to that first note."

"The notes and letters between you and your birth mother are important, but had you and your mother answered each other's letters, consider the possibilities," she offered. "The unanswered letters possibly hold the key to the weight on your chest. Answering her letters might have been your first white star in a bout with the sumo wrestler."

Eight

IN SURVIVAL MODE

*M*uch has been written about the inner world of adopted children and their unique development. Children are normally about two years old when they begin to be independent, but they always know that they can return to their mother or father if they are feeling unsafe. Adopted children in general do not have the security of retreating and must forge ahead. These children become hyper-vigilant and overly sensitive and spend an inordinate amount of time anticipating others' actions. Loyalty and recognition are important, and trust of others is taboo. For many, it is better to take total control over one's life, than to be abandoned again.

"Hence, having control over all things is critical for your safety net," says the Old Lady.

"Yes, Taking charge, ensuring I am safe, being responsible, doing my best, knowing what I need and being able to get it, pulling away, and walking away are key practices.

"I practice controlling only myself, but unknowingly these characteristics were spilling into my relationships. My brother and his family endearingly refer to me as "the bitch;" I am logical, organized, distant and independent."

"You mistakenly think that you're controlling only those things that involve you," says my long-time companion, "but that is not how 'having control' works. Having control is all-or-nothing. It usually involves other people and affects relations. As the late actress Katherine Hepburn said, 'In a relationship, when you win, you lose.'"

Total Control

After my adoptive mother died, I was relieved that my brother and I would not have to take care of our parents in their old age. I had forgotten that we had three lovely old aunts who never married. At the time, Aunt Lydie was 83 years old, Aunt Nettie, 89, and Aunt Clara, 93. The three lived together their entire lives, and their furniture, household and way of life were reminiscent of the early 1900s. They "paid" the neighborhood boy with a peach pie for cutting their grass, and their old friends always received boxes of homemade cookies or jars of fruit from their trees in appreciation for driving them to the doctors. They replaced the old broken things with new old; for a long time they looked to replace the old ringer washing machine with a new one. They worked the old- fashioned way; every week they were on their hands and knees cleaning the baseboards, washing the kitchen and bathroom floors, not missing a crack or corner.

But these charming anecdotes eventually turned into more serious signs of a need for assistance. During my visits, I heard an old friend responding sharply when Aunt Lydie asked her to drive her somewhere. The weeds were overgrown in the front and back yards. Aunts Clara and Nettie were stockpiling water from the washing machine and accidentally tripping over the buckets. Aunt Nettie was getting stuck between the refrigerator and the stove while cleaning, and the other two aunts could not get her out. They were taking turns in the hospital with broken hips and heart ailments. Eventually social workers from the hospital got wind of the three old ladies, and they started making visits.

My trips to Saint Charles became a cleaning session of the aunts' house. Every time I was there I removed old papers, emptied buckets, and slyly purged things that had no function or aesthetic value. My goal was to keep them in their home as long as possible. Invariably, a week after I had made a purge in the house, I received a letter from one of the aunts telling me that I had meddled in their lives. Aunt Nettie wrote a sweet, but direct letter,

It is always a joy to see you, my dearest . . . .

I save my buckets of water to soak the soil of the fruit trees. This year is bad for [some kind of] aphis, and the soapy water seems to protect the trees from unwanted bugs . . . . I am afraid that you threw out the water that I needed to rinse out my rags.

Aunt Lydie wrote the angriest letter, "Now you did it. You threw out our Advent wreath."

I remember the Advent wreath; it was an unadorned wire in the shape of a circle that had four small candle holders soldered equally distant on the wire; for it to be beautiful it needed the green garland, the pink and purple ribbons, and of, course, the candles. I saw it in the attic, and it remained there, but the aunts could not find it. Nonetheless, I was disruptive in the aunts' simple, honest lives.

The turning point was on my last visit to their house. As usual, the four of us were sitting at the dining room table talking about those who had died, which priests had been transferred, and who I didn't or did know. The doorbell rang, and I went to the door. My aunts' chiropractor stood at the door with his right arm curled around a tan metal card file box. He was a slender middle-aged man. He was also inebriated.

I stared at him for a few seconds, and finally said, "Yes?" He stared at me without a word.

Aunt Lydie finally spoke up, "Come in, Doctor."

He walked carefully in a straight line from the front door to the dining room table, and once he swayed to the right. He sat down and said, "It's time to be paid." *What an awkward way to collect for office visits*, as I deliberated.

None of the aunts said a word, and each of them lowered their heads. It dawned on me what was happening. I had the next and last words. I looked directly at the chiropractor and pointed at him, "You're drunk, *and* you're taking advantage of my aunts.

Get out *now*, and don't ever come here again." He left in silence, and the aunts did not say a word.

I had a sleepless night thinking about the inevitable. I knew that I had to find a nursing home for all aunts, and in one place. For 83 years Aunts Lydie and Nettie shared the same bedroom, and I would not change that. I spent the next day visiting nursing homes to inquire about the facilities. No organization was eager to take three sisters, and some recommended that I split them up, Aunts Lydie and Nettie in one place, and Aunt Clara in another.

When I started looking for nursing homes, Aunt Clara was already in a facility to recover after a hospital stay. First I approached Aunt Lydie, the head of the household. She barely was four feet eight inches tall; the osteoporosis stooped her over, and she painfully moved her bent neck to look up at me. She leaned against a doorway. I told her that it was time to move into an assisted living facility.

Her eyes began to water, and with a broken voice she said, "Perhaps it is time for the other two, but I will not think about it for another 10 years [93 years old]."

With courage that rented my heart, I replied, "No, if one goes, you all go." I knew how devastating that moment was, when three people totally lost control of their own lives, and I took complete control, not of my life, but of theirs.

It was clear that there was only one nursing home that would suit my aunts. It was three blocks away, and, most importantly, it was a Catholic institution. Mass was said at least once a day. The aunts also knew many of the residents. On the third day of searching, I spoke with the Carmelite Home administrator, Sister Mary Rose, about the circumstances, and she, too, was concerned about placing all three together. However, the nun was a kind, soft-spoken, compassionate woman with uncanny business acumen. She agreed to visit the aunts' home the following day. She talked with two of them. At the end of the next day Sr. Mary Rose telephoned me to tell me that Aunts Lydie and Nettie can continue to be roommates in one of their assisted living bedrooms, but they must go immediately. It was good news, but I abruptly asked, "And what about the third aunt?" I wanted to get Aunt Clara out of the current nursing home.

There was a long pause at the other end of the line, and she lowered her voice and said, "God will provide."

"What does that mean?" I asked.

"It might take a while," was Sr. Rose's response.

I should have been ecstatic, but I felt like I had just reached into my aunts' souls and torn out their remaining spirit and reason for living. That weekend Aunts Lydie and Nettie packed their bags and moved. They did not say a bad word to me, but I knew what I was doing to them.

I was on vacation for only two weeks, and my mission was to uproot and relocate my aunts. I took charge and made this monumental decision. My brother and his wife had been very helpful with the aunts, and they did as much as they could to keep them in their home. So, two aunts moved that weekend, and I had one more week in Saint Charles before returning to San Francisco to figure out what to do with the aunts' belongings, beautiful antique furniture, the house, and the third aunt. I originally told them that the house would remain intact, so that they did not feel like they were losing everything. However, realistically, if the house remained vacant, it would be vandalized.

To appease the aunts, I bought the house. They were happy knowing that their home was not sold to strangers. But to afford it, I needed to rent it. To rent it, I needed to move their furniture out and make some major repairs and improvements. During that one week, my brother and I brought our aunts to the house to help identify valuables. They rummaged through their belongings. There were no tears, but they were subdued. When Aunt Lydie became tired, she sat in the low lying white cherry rocking chair with her hands in her lap, her head tilted side-ways, watching us work.

I did not have time for an auction, and my brother was not predisposed to take on the responsibility for closing down the household. I contacted an antique dealer who was willing to take all the antiques and completely clean out the house. She offered $2500 for the antiques that I knew were worth at least 10 times that. I took the offer, but was ashamed of it. The day before the antique dealer came in with her crew, the aunts wanted to give certain things to friends and relatives. I had to remind them that I had already sold everything. I sat in their house late every night, smoking one cigarette after another, racking my brain for a better solution and for God (it was convenient to have Him in my corner) to give me the answer. I went to bed, tossed and turned, waking often and unable to get back to sleep. In a matter of days, I lost 13 pounds. For at least the next ten years I could not go into antique stores. Antiques reminded me of how I dismantled the lives of three kind, precious people in a very short time.

By the end of the second week, hours before I was to return to my home in San Francisco, all three aunts were together at the Carmelite Home. On the first Sunday in the senior facility, we went to Mass together. I was pleased that they were together doing what they enjoyed most — practicing their religion. At the kiss of peace, I kissed and shook hands with Aunt Lydie, and she squeezed my hand so tightly that it hurt; my ring left a long-lasting indentation in my pinky finger. Her strength was daunting, and as I looked into her tear-filled eyes, I realized that her grip was a release of the emotion she was feeling. Later that day I said good-bye to each of them. No one blamed me or treated me with disdain. All gave me passionate good-byes, not necessarily because it might be the last time they would see me, but because their hearts were full with hurt and loss. I promised myself never again to take control of someone else's life. It was, at best, gut-wrenching.

Throughout my life I have envied people who knew from where they had come, were content with their lot in life, and lived every day as though it were a good day. My aunts' hands were always busy, and their minds were always focused upward toward Heaven. My aunts were simple, gentle little women; they had no facades and no unkind words. I hope that God gave them the front pew in Heaven.

No Control

My second lesson in control came shortly after the last aunt died, when I was diagnosed with squamous cell cancer of the unknown primary site (CUPS). The cancer metastasized, and I had a slim chance for survival. For almost five months before the diagnosis I went to numerous, varying medical specialists to determine why I had pain in my lower back and the left groin area. I was disheartened by the medical field, and finally expressed it to an orthopedic doctor, who, after I had given him a lecture on compassion, had mercy on me, and offered to biopsy the lymph nodes in the groin. I was preparing for a business trip to North Dakota on the day that the doctor telephoned me to say: "As an orthopedic doctor, I don't give this type of news; so, I don't know how else to say this: You have cancer."

The oncologist and the radiologist, both knowledgeable and compassionate, immediately sent me to numerous specialists to determine the original site. They found nothing. After a while, I told the radiologist, "Until the doctors start treatment, I have no hope." In front of me, she telephoned the oncologist to tell him that they need a treatment despite not knowing the origin. At the next local Tumor Board they discussed the medical results and protocol.

My treatment was rigorous: maximal in-patient chemotherapy, maximal radiation, surgeries, and lots of nausea and vomiting. I was most humiliated when standing with family and friends and losing control of my bowels. I was ashamed, like the child who wet the bed. Like others with this disease, I stood in the shower to wash my hair, and clumps of hair came out in my hands. When I tried to remove the hair from my hands, my legs buckled, and I fell to my knees and started crying. My future husband Michael heard me fall, and ran into the bathroom. Without a word he turned off the sprinkler, and gently raised me to my feet and held me. He then sat me on the toilet seat, removed the hair from my hands, dried me off and dressed me.

"Lay down. I'll fix you something to eat."

He came back with a small slice of beef and spinach. I tried to eat, but I felt myself becoming nauseous. I quickly grabbed the pail next to my bed and vomited. Michael picked up the plate of food. "I'll fix you something else."

He returned 20 minutes later with oatmeal, but I looked at it, and it reminded me too much of the vomit. I looked into Michael's eyes, and without a word he scooped up the bowl of oatmeal and the vomit pail. He returned shortly with chicken and rice and a clean vomit pail.

"Thank you, Michael," but he did not answer me. Instead, he went into the bathroom to measure and record my outputs and intakes.

He moved me into his home to watch over and feed me. At the time I was diagnosed, Michael was renovating the inside of his home, and he intentionally worked on the room next to my bedroom so that he could hear me when I called for help. He never left my side throughout that critical period. My fiancé stuck me with needles and rigged ladders for my blood transfusions. He held my hand when I curled up into a ball. I assumed he was going to leave me, but he was never farther than a few steps from me. I mulled over all the horror stories of other men leaving their wives and girlfriends because they did not know how to handle cancer. Michael went to all my doctors' appointments with me. He visited me twice daily during my five hospital stays, and made sure that someone was with me 24 hours a day when I was not in the hospital. In my quest to be wanted, I became certain of Michael's undying love. Michael was the reason I wanted to survive.

At my lowest point with cancer, I was on the verge of kidney failure. The doctors did not think I was going to live. I was dangerously dehydrated, and neither solids nor liquids stayed in me. My hospital roommate was a brain tumor patient whose head was completely shaven. At night she had nightmares, and during the day she hallucinated. She was tethered to the bed. Her visiting family members argued with her regularly. A couple of times Michael complained to the nurses and once confronted my roommate's husband that I was very sick, and they were upsetting me. As I became weaker, the noise scared me; I knew that my roommate was about to die, and I was next.

In the middle of the last night that I was with my roommate, she dropped a glass, which shattered to the four corners of the room. I had chronic diarrhea and needed to get to a bathroom. I rang and rang for assistance, and no one answered. I did not want to get out of bed because of the glass on the floor. Finally, my bowels took charge, and I lay in my own waste. In humiliation and anger, I yanked the call bell out of the wall. If it served no purpose, it shouldn't be in my room. Everything in my life at this point had to have a meaning, and that call bell was useless. I wept for at least five hours. A nurse's aide eventually came to my bed side to clean my mess. She ruthlessly scrubbed my sensitive skin with a coarse, white wash cloth to a point where I was feeling physically abused. I wanted to slap her hand away from my body, but my body itself felt like a lifeless rag. My mind insisted that I needed to stop her, but the same hands that tore out an industrial strength call bell, could not do this one small useful thing. Michael visited that morning and saw how distressed I was. He told the attending doctor that he could take better care of me than the hospital staff. The doctor disagreed, but he also discharged me from the hospital with the caveat that I would be back within two days.

When Michael returned from signing the release papers, I was locked in the fetal position. I hated being in the hospital, but I was afraid to leave. Nurses and a social worker talked to me to no avail. Finally, Michael gently started changing me into street clothes. He put a diaper on me first. About five miles down the road, I filled my diaper, and we stopped twice on the side of the road for me to vomit. After a few minutes, I asked, "How bad was the call bell?"

"You did a number on it. Not to worry. You have made a name for yourself at the hospital."

I laughed.

During treatment, I said at least two times a day to my fiancé, "All I want is to be normal, to feel well, just for an hour." It seemed like I never was going to get well; the pain, nausea, fogginess, tiredness and needles seemed endless. Time stopped. The days all ran together. I must have looked at the calendar, but never registered that days were passing.

I placed one foot in front of the other, blindly. Colleagues admired me for the courage I exhibited while going through the treatment. I wondered, "What's to admire? I have no control, not over my body or mind. They do what they want. If I throw up or lose control of my bowels — what's to admire? I do what I have to do." Perhaps they were unconsciously relieved that it was me and not them, not knowing if they could face being that sick. However, there were innumerable times, when I wanted to give up all treatment just to have a few hours of feeling normal and healthy.

One of the standard "feel-good" methods of fighting cancer is imaging, which is the manipulation of a mental picture. In my case, the social workers tried to get me to visualize a place where I felt at home, and where I could comfortably fight the cancer cells, much like imagining Packman going through my body and destroying all the bad cells. I tried visualizing the game hero being aggressive and eating the bad cells quicker than they could reproduce. Some of the time I won the game -- eating up the cancer cells before they ate me. Most of the time, I found my mind wandering to other topics, such as, "Dear Lord, will I beat this?" Oh, so now that I need a God, I believe in one? The most desolate feeling was to lie in bed at night and silently cry to God for help, and in the same moment to remember that I struggled with the concept of God. That's when I realized how dependent I was on someone or something other than myself, and reliance on other men, regardless of their expertise, was not enough.

The social workers gave patients a tape recording of soothing music that was conducive to imaging. I played it constantly, trying to find that "special place." Eventually, I settled on a lake in the Cascade Mountains, ironically named Lake Valhalla, which peaked in a waterfall and gushed down the mountain. All the people from whom I wanted support, dead or alive, were standing at that narrow point, looking at me with glowing faces of encouragement. My adoptive father, brother, aunts, grandmother, Mothers Marheineke and Tainter, a surrogate mother and her sister, a handful of friends, and all the people who had sent me get-well cards and telephoned me were there. I never had such a large group of people cheering me. My adoptive mother was not there. My mind studied each face, and, eventually, after reviewing these faces almost daily, I realized that they were giving me hope.

The Old Lady looks down on me, "What will your death be like?"

"Death is for the dead. Life is for the living. Right now I must live one day at a time." I talk a good story. I don't believe in life after death, and I obsess with death. "Every day during treatment I try to contemplate what's important in life, but I get no further than hoping I am wrong about not having a life after death." I add as an afterthought, "I'm also struggling with having no legacy."

She hesitated on the word legacy. "Nearly every village has its own cemetery. How many graves haven't had visitors for decades?" My friend seems to be pondering her own questions. "How many of those people are still remembered?"

"To be remembered is important to me. It's the only way I can feel that I have a purpose on this earth." Both the Old Lady and I are quiet for a few minutes. I continue, "Dante's Inferno is an obtuse reminder that what one does on this earth is the penultimate chapter. Dante placed in Heaven some notorious people, and in Hell some renowned good people, such as some of the saints, popes, and even Virgil. Some people in Hell practiced good, but not for the sake of goodness. They met a selfish need. That bolsters

the Women's Self-Help Center colleague's remark about teetotalers and questioning their ulterior motives. Some people fail to practice good by omission only. According to you, when you talk about sins of omission, I should be going to Hell. In essence, though, our life on earth begins and ends in practicing good, and that is the final reward."

"Do you really believe that? Most of those forgotten dead lived their lives in hopes of something better after life." The Old Lady continues, changing the topic slightly, *"Most of them had children, and that is their legacy. And you?"*

"Before I began the treatment, the radiologist informed me that the radiation would make me infertile. Let me think about that: I have a chance to live with treatment, and I have no chance without it.

"Yet, women are expected to marry and have children. My adoptive mother might have been a slave to that social expectation, even though she might have had no desire to be a mother. For years I've wrestled with whether to have a child or adopt, but I am always put off by my fears, primarily the fear of harming the child more than if the child remained under the care of a state facility.

"And I worry about the 'what ifs,' the worry and self-doubt. What if I treat my child the way I was treated? What if I give the child only discipline and no affection? What if I don't give enough time to my child? Would giving the child a house with a babysitter be better than no home at all? The purpose of adopting is to give children a family, to give them a loving, nurturing, safe environment, not to give the adoptive parents a loving, nurturing, safe environment."

*"Have you become who you are because you were adopted?
Because of the way you were raised? Or have you chosen how to
react to life?" asks the Old Lady.*

*I respond with more questions. "At what point are children
capable of being proactive and taking responsibility for their own
actions? How long can people blame their behavior on what happened to them as children? How long can they be victims?"*

*"Human brains are unique. They have capabilities and emo-
tions that are propelled by attachment from the moment of concep-
tion, and more clearly through warmth and affection after birth.
Perhaps a mother's touch and protection is the fuel that awakens
emotions like compassion, selflessness, and bonding with others.
Without the fuel, the capabilities and emotions are not developed.
The picture of a mother and child together is the ultimate sign
of love and warmth, not because it is any woman and child, but
because it is a mother who loves and develops the child's brain so
the child may learn how to love. If those parts of the brain are not
developed, the only thing the child has learned is survival. If that is
true, a child in survival mode will react until her death."*

*I am impressed with the Old Lady's memory of my books,
but she was telling me that I'm a woman in survival mode, and
because I was not taught how to love, I would not be able to teach
a child. "So, if I conceive a child AND change myself completely,
I have a chance. If I adopt a child, I still must change to have a
chance! Perhaps I have made the right decision — to do nothing."*

*"You have let fear guide you," the wise Old Lady says. "There's no
truth in what you said. Fear torments you. You over-think, ruminate
like a cow, and manufacture scenarios. You fear abandonment and*

you fear disappointing someone. Think of your shadow family, and how the possibility of a child is now only a star. Think of how your life might have been."

"One minute you tell me that my brain has not developed and I am incapable of knowing attachment and care, and now you tell me that fear rules. Think of all the adults who were abused as children. When the police and social workers interview parents of abused children, they learn the parents are often the same people who swore not to abuse their children as they were abused."

"Fear does rule you. Children are born in survival mode, and fear is a major part of survival. Children unlearn fear because their mother offers love and security. If a mother is not present, the child's fear becomes adult-like, and it is difficult to reverse that emotion."

Through my long sickness, the fellow FBI employees "covered" for me, allowed me "to work" at home, and made sure that if my fiancé could not care for me for some reason, someone from the office came to sit with me. The assistant director told the FBI Academy nurse to take whatever time she needed to help me. A well-known speaker that I had contracted for management presentations at the FBI Academy wanted to give Michael and me a trip around the world. We could not accept it because it would have been a conflict of interest, but his generous offer was gift enough. I have saved all the cards and get well wishes since 1994 to remind me of the outpouring of love and care shown to me.

The oncologist and radiologist were vigorously looking for the site of cancer origin, because knowing the site determined the kind of treatment; not knowing the site meant the medical professionals had to guess. A medical history could help identify the original site. My colleague, with whom I shared an office, contacted the FBI Legal Attaché in Bonn, Germany to find my birth mother to get a medical history. I gave him an old address. The Special Agents in Germany made contact with my mother, but, according to the investigators, she could not help much. She said that her mother had died early in middle age of some kind of disease, but she couldn't name it. I was excited to learn that my mother was still living and in the same place, and that there was again a thin thread of contact between us, but I was so single-minded on, and overwhelmed by, my fight to physically survive, that I could not enjoy the full impact of knowing that my birth mother knew that I was in trouble.

The most striking thing I learned from being sick, besides having control taken completely out of my hands, was what it was like to be totally focused. When I worked on my Ph.D. dissertation, I was similarly centered. However, during the dissertation process I kept telling myself that there was more to life than work and the dissertation. When I was sick, there was nothing more to life. While other people groused about work, grocery shopping, troubled relationships and so on, I felt a freedom from all that. I was impervious. National and world news, normally my passion, did not interest me. None of that had any meaning to my life. In exchange, I saw people in a more humane light, with more compassion. I also looked at trees and skies differently; colors were more vivid.

I tried to be engaged and go to work at the FBI Academy at least a couple of hours each day, but as the treatment progressed, I became weaker, was continually nauseated, and could hardly stand. At first Michael took me to work every day, and walked with me around the outdoor track once or twice. He waited for me while I puttered around the office, and then drove me home. On one such occasion, Attorney General Janet Reno was giving a presentation to all the Special Agents in Charge at the FBI Academy, and she used me as an example of commitment. I was unaware of that until days later. However, on that day that she and I were both at the Academy, one of FBI Director Louis Freeh's protective staff walked into my office to ask if I were available for a visit from the Director and the Attorney General. Minutes later both Freeh and Reno walked into my office. Janet Reno was an inch away from having to lower her head to get through the doorway. I sent a thank-you note to both officials for spending valuable time with me, and both responded with handwritten notes.

While I was receiving warm wishes and offers of help, and after I realized how difficult it was to get through the treatment, I wondered what would have happened to me if Michael had not offered to take care of me day and night. Michael and I had known each other for only five months. Who else would have taken on the engulfing task? Would I have stopped the treatment if I had not had someone as forceful as Michael to guide me? An older friend had offered to take care of me, but she would have relented to my pleas to not eat, shower, move from bed, or go to treatments. I believe, given the nature of the cancer, I would have been dead. Had I not met Michael, I would have wanted to die.

The stark reality was that I was a puppet alone with what appeared to be my imminent death, and Michael, along with the medical professionals, held those strings that were humanly available. But I sensed they didn't hold all the strings. My fiancé and I talked about whether there was a God.

"I believe there is a Supreme Being," Michael said. "You?"

"Right now, I must believe. I have a five to 15 percent chance of surviving. But every time I think about God, I grow somber, because if there is a God, then I have hurt him -- whatever God is—and I always equate hurt to the horrific weight on my chest. How can I ask anything of anyone that I have hurt? I'm a dead woman, aren't I?"

Michael never liked to talk about death. Instead, he said, "It's time," and he pulled out the rosary. Every night during the treatment we said the rosary together, just in case.

Two weeks after my last treatment, I woke up and realized it was spring. I looked at the calendar and for the first time since I was diagnosed, it registered what day it was. A month after the last chemo treatment I was back to work. I started to run and lift weights again, and I began to feel normal. Normal, though, meant worrying about unimportant things and being stressed over matters that were not life threatening. Normal meant the return of the sumo wrestler, always a champion with a winning technique that takes the air from my lungs and presses my chest into the ring.

The Old Lady and I have not talked during most of the medical treatment period; I had been absorbed primarily with fighting a foe that was far more elusive than the sumo wrestler. Over the last 12 months I had little energy or concentration to read or study. Today, though, is a good day. I walk into my office, and my eyes beat as they concentrate on the hundreds of books, trinkets, and wall hangings. The sight of the red, bright blue, green, and orange book covers are an alarming splash of cold water in the face. "Hello, Old Lady!"

She gives me her usual welcoming grin. "Hello, my child."

"It's good to be back—and alive."

"It's good to have you back—and alive."

"As I was going through the cancer treatment and after the surgeon gave me less than five years to live, I understood alone. The last five years of my life were going to be with people who would be totally clueless—until it was their time—of what I was thinking or feeling. I'd rather be alone. I sat at restaurant tables with chirpy people who were intent on cheering me up and including me in discussions of shopping, funny television shows, and work. My mind wandered to my legacy, not being a part of this world for long, and desperately searching for what's still important. My gaze seemed far off; as I looked at my well-wishers, my eyes went through them and beyond to an incomprehensible world of a person who contemplated her final destination. And, of course, I would die alone. All those

childhood years that I felt alone, and all I really wanted was to be either understood or accepted."

I close my eyes for couple minutes in hopes that when I reopen them the colors and light will be more subdued.

For a short time, I made a point of appreciating the small things in life. My runs around the quiet roads of the FBI Academy usually ended with gratitude to a Supreme Being that I could enjoy the run and experience being alive. For a couple years I ingratiated myself to the same Being, assuming that if God knows I am grateful, He will never give me cancer again. Of course, the tension in my chest increased as I became less focalized on the task of staying alive. I was still looking for answers without knowing the questions, but I once again took total control, as any good prison warden would.

Another Missed Opportunity

In 1998, after I had completed my work assignment in Budapest, I took a side trip to Germany. I stayed in a hotel in the small, picturesque village, Traben-Trarbach, on the Mosel River, not far from Wittlich and Minderlittgen. I wanted the feel of the area where my birth mother had lived, and to imagine what my life would have been like, had I been raised by her. The sites of the vineyards on the steep hills that led to the river offered a natural high. I envied my mother, her having lived amidst the prehistoric volcanic Eifel Mountains and the ancient Mosel River. I wondered whether she enjoyed her surroundings, regardless of how difficult her life might have been.

I decided it was time to venture back to my natural mother's village, to do some "drive-bys," in the jargon of law enforcement. As I approached the village, I suddenly became sick to my stomach. I stopped on the side of the road, just before the entrance to the village to vomit. After a time, I drove slowly through Minderlittgen, and parked at an angle so that I could see the house. I sat there for about 10 minutes, and noticed that older ladies were looking out their windows, probably wondering who I was. Still honoring my promise to my mother not to let anyone in her village know of my existence, I quickly left my parking spot. I found another spot to survey her house, and was there only a few minutes when I saw someone come out of her home — a woman, younger than my mother. I became jittery and drove away. If I had a better command of German, I might have defied my mother's wishes and knocked on her door.

My mind was filled with questions on the trip back to the hotel: Was my mother dead? Did she no longer live there? Was the woman a relative?

The next day I bought a bottle of white wine and some cheese, and I trekked up a steep vineyard path. At the peak were a small cemetery and a chapel. I sat with my wine and cheese, and I drank out of the bottle. I had almost finished the wine before I realized I hadn't eaten any cheese, which would have made me less drunk. My head was swimming, and my digestive system was churning. I needed a lavatory, and the only thing available was more nature behind the chapel, next to the vineyard. I was grateful for the large vine leaves. But on the next day after driving 200 kilometers to the Frankfurt Airport, I realized that I had dropped my driver's license and credit cards on that same spot behind the chapel.

"Another missed opportunity," the Old Lady said, uninvited.
"Yes. I was afraid."

Part Three

Nine

DISCOVERING THE SHADOW FAMILY

An e-mail changed my life. In 2010, I was doing a quick review of e-mails and almost deleted one that had sneaked through my spam filter. It was from Matthias Merkl and had a foreign address; I smelled a scam. The caption began, "Hi, Mrs. Malone . . . ." Scam. I reached for the mouse to click and delete, but while I was doing that I read the rest of the subject: "Hi, Mrs. Malone, do you have a mother in Germany, this is no joke." The words, "this is no joke" was another sign that I should delete the e-mail, but I did have a mother in Germany. I was intrigued. It was written in English:

Hello, Mrs. Malone,

My name is Matthias Merkl from Germany, Wittlich, and my grandmother is Mathilde Violett, Minderlittgen, may be your mother, because I have a letter written in 1998 in which a Marita Malone is writing to her. My mother, Sofia Merkl, gave it to me a few time ago, an so I was searching for Marita Malone who worked for the FBI in former times an lived in Virginia in 1998. I hope that you are the right Marita Malone. I would be glad if it is so. My mother heard just one year ago that my grandmother had another child which was given away, so she asked me to search for this other daughter, please just say if you are the right one an if you serious. If you do not believe me, just call me on 049 . . . .

I must have read that e-mail a hundred times before acting on it. My emotions raced from disbelief to ecstasy. Because I had never heard from my half-sister or -brother, I assumed that either my birth mother never told them about me, or she had, and they had no interest in knowing me.

With restraint I replied that my mother was Mathilde Violett, and I wanted to meet my half-sister and her son Matthias and his wife Rita. Matthias responded that my mother still lived, and he sent a lovely picture of my elderly, albeit healthy mother, who was ambulatory with a walker. He also stated:

. . My mum is still so happy that you were the right one [in Matthias' Internet search], and she's asking about you, sitting in front of your photo an wondering why this all happened. She went to my grandmother to tell her the news and my grandma was happy that you were found, she told my mother that in former times she did not want to have

contact between you and her other children because she was
ashamed of having given you away. . . .

That same e-mail delivered the news that my half-brother had
died a few years earlier.

A series of messages flew between Matthias and me, mostly talking of the excitement of my mother and half-sister over finding me.
But we also shared family histories. When he asked his mother what
she would like to say to me, she said, "Leaving Germany was the best
that could happen to you." Sofia had a hard childhood. Her father
left my mother with two children, and they survived in a small village during and after World War II. My mother, with her limited
resources, typically favored the son and did what she could to further
his career. Eventually, there was a family dispute, and Sofia did not
speak to our mother for many years. In 2007, when Matthias and
Rita were getting married, Rita insisted that Matthias' grandmother
be invited. My mother was happy to join her family again. Later,
when my mother became terminally ill, Sofia was with her.

A few e-mails later, Matthias sent me a photo of my mother,
half-sister, and him and his wife at their wedding. My mother
was sitting. In contrast to the first photo, she had lost a lot of
weight, and had a large, flesh-colored bandage over the left side
of her face. Her hair was shaved back midway, as though she had
had surgery, and the rest of her hair was thin and straight. She
had cancer. I then looked closely at the first photo, in which she
looked healthy, and I saw faint dark spots all over her otherwise
porcelain face. Later, I received a message from Rita that my birth

mother was falling, had a blood clot in her head, and needed another surgery. I realized it was urgent to see her.

I had been thinking about waiting to go to Germany at Christmas time. Saint Louis University was just beginning the new academic year, and I was doing what I do best—thinking about my work before relationships. If I were to wait until Christmas, would my 88-year old mother still be alive? Was this another opportunity that I was throwing away? I have, after all, lived with the regret of failing to tell my adoptive father that I loved him. I have lived with the regret that I selfishly chose time for myself over visiting my favorite aunt before she died. What if I missed this last opportunity with my birth mother?

I decided to travel to Germany immediately and meet some of my shadow family.

I look up at the Old Lady. She has nothing to say.

Ten

THAT PEACEFUL PLACE

Two Sides to Every Truth

Minderlittgen has been traced back to 912 A.D., when it was called Lutiaco. There are signs of the Romans before that time. Near the village is Trier, the oldest city in Germany that still has remains of Roman buildings during Caesar's era. Until 1147, St. Maximin's Abbey was the landholder of Lutiaco. Afterwards, it was governed by Trier electorates, only under the name of Minoris Lideche. Slowly, in 1503, thanks to the Minderlittgen dialect of Mosel-Franko, the name evolved into Minnerlietge, and today Minderlittgen (Günter Hesse, 1989, *Minderlittgen: Geschickte einer Berggemeinde im Wittlicher Land*). Many Luxembourgians had migrated to the area after the Black Plague, not because they wanted to go there, but because they themselves were infected and were part of a diaspora from Luxembourg and France. When tourists drive through the countryside, history comes alive as they see churches built in the 1300s about a half mile away from the villages. Cemeteries were physically next to churches, and having deceased plague victims too close to the villages to contaminate others was precluded by building the churches away from the village.

After the plague was no longer a threat, the villagers built their homes around the churches, with the roofs and steeples soaring to the heavens. The old churches were massive on the outside, but surprisingly small inside. The ceilings of the stone buildings were painted in intricate religious artwork, and the interior walls were painted to mimic stone blocks laid one upon the other. Directly across the narrow street from my mother's early 1800s home was the Minderlittgen village church that had been built on a small hill to make it even more prominent.

Until approximately the mid-1900s, the homes had no street name or address. Instead, many homes were identified by the occupation of the homeowner. The metal worker, who molded horse and cow shoes, lived in the *Schmiedshaus,* the house of the iron worker; and *Schreiner Otto's* house was where a carpenter had lived, and the first name of Otto was the current owner. In some homes the family adopted the last name of the man's vocation. Hence, Josef Schumacher is Joseph Shoe Maker. Other homes were named after the person who built the house. The name of my mother's house was Konrad Tilli; my grandmother's maiden name was Konrad, and the house was built by her family. Tilli was my mother's nickname.

As late as the early 1970s, only about 120 houses plus barns were in the village. Minderlittgen was typical old Europe, where the people lived in close clusters and the barns were attached to their houses. In most cases, the barns were much larger than the homes and built with the same discerning care. The farmland surrounded the villages. Each day the villagers left their homes with their cultivators, tractors and workhorses, and they often worked together in the fields. Inside the barns were their equipment, pigs, cows, workhorses, chickens, and, often, the family bath water and outhouse. Night-visit pots were under their beds and emptied daily. Many houses did not have modern conveniences until the late 1960s and early 1970s. My mother did not have a modern toilet and bathroom until 1976. Today the village has grown considerably, housing approximately 900 people, but only one villager is still tilling the fields.

"Before you go to Europe, I want to tell you a story," The Old Lady always knows what I am up to. "A mule that never really worked a day in his life spent the days in a pasture. He was feeling particularly frisky on this day, and decided that he was going to run as fast as he could. He told others, 'My mother was a race horse.' He challenged himself to run as fast as she. Not long after, the farmer needed to get into town quickly, and he jumped on the mule, but the mule was not going fast enough. The farmer cajoled and beat the animal to go faster. Finally, the breathless mule gasped, 'You don't understand. My mother was a race horse, but my father was only a jackass.' Remember, my dear, that every truth has two sides."

"Thank you, my friend," I respond warmly.

Sofia's Truth

In the first week of August 2010, I flew to Frankfurt and drove to the Moseltal (the valley of the Mosel River) in the western part of Germany. Like most parts of Europe, the Mosel River was a passageway for the Romans, Teutonic tribes, and other invaders. Monuments, forts, and castles are still nestled in the steep hillsides that were carved by the river and the molten volcanic fires tens of thousands of years ago. Today the rocky mountainside is covered with miles of vineyards. While driving from the Frankfurt Airport, the landscape transformed from the flat big city to rolling hills and villages to steep hills and volcanic heights. Eventually, I drove down a steep, winding, forested hill toward the Mosel. At the bottom of the hill was picturesque Bernkastel. This historic town, along with Trier, was the showcase of the area in which I was born. My heart started to pound.

Farther up the river, I parked my car in the small hotel parking lot adjacent to the river. I sat for only seconds, when a woman with short blonde hair and a camera came up to the car and took a picture of me through the windshield. I wondered aloud, "Am I illegally parked in this spot? I'm sorry, but I don't read German that well. Okay, okay. I'll move." I took a quick glance at the sign in front of my vehicle for parking directions and was about to restart the motor of the car, when I realized that this woman was my half-sister. She had been sitting in her car waiting for me.

I reacted uncharacteristically by jumping out of the car and embracing her. We could not speak each other's language, but that made no difference. We walked to her car, where she pulled out two champagne glasses and a small bottle of Sekt. (I did not know until later that she had accidentally broken a first bottle in her car, and it smelled like a vintner's cellar.) We sat on a bench on the bank of the Mosel and stared at each other.

"You are like your father, small build and facial features." My sister was first to speak. I had always assumed since I was 23 years old that I resembled my mother. I had never even considered what my father looked like. Sofia continued, "He still lives in the village."

That was an unexpected incoming bomb. Both of my biological parents were still living. All these years I had supposed they were dead. As a child, I had envisioned my birth father as a tall, strong man, much like my German nephews Matthias and Sasha, with chiseled jaws and piercing eyes. I had concocted a story of my mother and he having a tryst during a difficult time in history, a moment of happiness and pleasure in an otherwise bleak existence. But I never reflected upon my father beyond that. I always accepted my deceased adoptive father as the one male figure in my life, the one who protected me. That's what fathers are supposed to do, isn't it? Besides, I assumed that my birth father had no interest in me and did not want his family to know. Like my birth mother's secret, it was my father's secret, too; it was the only thing all three of us had in common.

Later in the day, Sofia, along with her son and daughter-in-law, returned to the hotel. We drove along the meandering Mosel and passed one wine village after another. Healthy, picture-perfect grape vines hung between buildings, and the flowers, plentiful and sweet, adorned the gardens and houses. We stopped at a typical German restaurant, a 1400s building of wattle-and-daub infilled white plaster panels with an exposed brown timber frame, known as a half-timber building. The ceilings were low and the interior rustic. It was a lovely introduction into Sofia's world. I gave Sofia a necklace of two keys, one yellow gold and the other white gold, on a gold chain, symbolic of the two daughters and our mother's unlocked secret. I will never know if she understood the significance of that gift.

We were barely seated when Sofia said, "When I was a child, our mother angrily pulled my hair because I would not polish my shoes. That is what I remember of my mother."

"My American mother pulled my hair also, and that is what I remember of her," I returned. Silence at the table.

"My mother did everything for my brother. We never had any money. She saved to get my brother an education and all the opportunities, within her limitations, and he became a butcher instead. I was not allowed to go to school after a few years. Nothing was done for me."

Matthias added, "Mother, on her own steam, got her educational certificate."

I flashed back to my childhood story. I did not know how to tell her that my American mother worked for my brother's education, without sounding like I was mimicking her and taking away from the value of what she said. I also remembered one of the Old Lady's fables when I was feeling sorry for myself; misery loves company. So instead, I said, "It seems that you and I were stuck in the tail end of an era when the son gets everything and the daughter is expected to stay home and do housework." *How trite,* I deemed. We both knew that was no excuse for denying opportunities to girls. There was silence at the table.

"Without telling our mother, I left the house when I was 16, and went into the small town of Wittlich to get my first job as a waitress. We had no father, and I did not want to grow up like our mother, milking cows and cleaning houses for the rest of my life." Although Sofia returned home every night, she was taking her first steps to independence. She was choosing to change what she believed to be a repressive lifestyle.

My mind wandered momentarily. As a child, I had constantly wondered if I would have been milking cows had I stayed in Germany. Silence again.

"For most of my life I did not call our mother *Mutter,* mother, or *Mutti,* mom" she said. "I called her by her first name, Tilli."

I did not respond, but my brother John and I never called our American mother anything but the formal Mother. We were informal with our father, Daddy. While I waited for Sofia to speak again, I speculated on whether or not we, as children, chose those salutations for our parents, or if the parents decided for us what they wanted to be called.

Sofia finished, "Our mother's sister-in-law was more of a mother to me than Tilli." I could tell by Sofia's staccato remarks that our first dinner meeting was not a good time to pry, much less to ask any heavy questions.

"I took several different jobs as a waitress. I met my ex [former husband], and we ran a roofing business together. Things were pretty good. We traveled outside of Europe." More silence.

Sofia decided to continue, "I remembered when I was a child, an infant was in the house, and I thought that I was only dreaming. One day you were there, and the next day you were gone. No one in the village ever spoke of it, and eventually the dream faded." I had a sharp intake of breath. Sofia remembered me as a baby! The sumo wrestler suddenly weighed less. I was part of her family, and I could envision Sofia, my mother and others bustling around me in their kitchen.

I asked what otherwise would have a simple, safe answer. "Were our grandparents good people?"

"*Ja*, but I did not like what my grandmother did to Tilli. When our mother told her that she was pregnant with you, I saw my grandmother pick up a sharp knife and throw it at my mother. I did not know what 'pregnant' meant at the time, but I vividly remember the knife being thrown." Sofia had deep-seeded care, if not duty, or even a convoluted love, for our mother.

"Shortly before you were born, I was sent away to live with Aunt Elke in Frankfurt until after you were born. I was only six years old. Aunt Elke and her husband lived across the street from the orphanage. After you were born, Aunt Elke took you from Minderlittgen to the orphanage. They once drove back to the village to visit my mother and grandparents, and you were in the back seat, but you were not allowed to get out of the car. Our mother stood at the front door of the house and looked at you.

"Aunt Elke told me that when Tilli was pregnant with you, she was working as a cleaning lady in Wittlich, about six kilometers from her village. She began to have birthing pains and went to the local hospital, but she was not ready to deliver. By the time Tilli was released from the hospital, the busses were no longer running for the day, and she walked home, more than 6 kilometers, on a winding, dangerous road. Shortly after our mother had arrived home, she was definitely due, and she was rushed back to the hospital." Pause. I later supposed my mother walked in the dark on a cold December day the 19 dangerous switchbacks in the road from Wittlich to Minderlittgen, or the uneven cow paths up the steep hills to the village.

"My father was only a *Samenspender*, a sperm donor," Sofia offered. He went back to Austria without my mother. I heard that I have many half-brothers and -sisters from him."

I said nothing. My biological father was also just a sperm donor, but now that I knew he was still alive, I was going to see him, somehow.

The first evening with my half-sister ended, and I was exhausted. I went to my hotel room, immediately undressed and climbed into bed. I tossed and turned, but it did not lead to sleep. I was grateful when daylight came.

My Birth Mother's Truth

When I went to my half-sister's apartment, the first thing Sofia asked was, "Did you sleep well?"

"No," I answered. I could tell by her look that neither had she.

We climbed into her car and drove to my mother's village. Matthias had hired a translator, and she was waiting, sitting outside my mother's house, smoking a cigarette. We greeted each other and walked up the stairs into my mother's house. I had gone up those stairs only one time before, when I was an infant coming home from the hospital. Fifty-nine years later I entered the same, mostly unchanged house.

My mother waited in what had been her tiny living room now converted into a convalescent room. She sat in an armchair, behind a walker. She wore a crisp, light green blouse with an immaculate, white sweater, and a dark green skirt. On her temples were large tumors and unhealed sores. Her hairline was still shaved back. Her smile was lop-sided from nerve damage due to a bad surgery. To me, my mother was beautiful.

I had asked my mother if she minded that Sofia stay while I ask questions, and she agreed. So, the three of us and the translator sat in the small room. I showed my mother a little photo album of my life. I asked her to talk about her childhood, and she did not say much. I asked her to talk about many things that would not offend my mother or Sofia, but most of the conversation did not go far. She was a woman of very few words. I tried talking about the German history during the time of Sofia's and my birth, but she did not say much about that either. She talked about being relegated to the cellar during World War II when the American soldiers took over the family house, but I spent most of my time looking at her strong hands and her eyes, and she did not take her sore eyes off me.

My mother insisted that we have coffee and cake. Shortly after her grandson and Sofia's nephew, Sasha, entered the room. He did not say a word to anyone. He had come at an unusual hour to help my mother with her pills. It was clear he had heard that I was coming, and he wanted to see me. Because no one else was talking to him, I did not introduce myself. I was in my mother's house and village, and I did not want to stir up the *Dorfgespraech*, village talk. We sat in awkward silence. Later in the day I learned that my sister Sofia and her son Matthias had a disagreement with Sasha and his family, and they did not speak to one another.

The other intriguing event during this first visit was that someone from my father's house had walked down the street to my mother's and asked to see me. Sofia shooed him away because it was the boyfriend of my father's daughter, and she did not think that was appropriate. I agreed with Sofia. I was, after all, a guest of Sofia and in my mother's house.

After about two hours, I was alone with my mother and I kissed her good-bye. She asked when I was coming back to her. It stunned me. Why wouldn't I return to visit her? Why did I assume I would not see her again? I quickly recovered from my surprise, and told her, "I will visit again."

My mother was not satisfied with a general answer. "*Wann,* when?" she asked. I was shocked that she wanted to see me again. I wanted to see her, too, but by this time in my life, I learned to live with my feeling of wanting more and settling for less.

Sofia paid the translator, and we drove off and joined Matthias and Rita for lunch, but my thoughts were only of my mother. Later in the evening when in my hotel room, I paced the floor furiously for more than an hour. I went to bed, and again mapped the entire bed with a million tosses and turns. Each night I failed to sleep, and each day Sofia, despite already knowing the answer, asked me if I'd slept well.

Three days later, we again met the translator outside my mother's house, but this time Sofia and I had an animated discussion about living in the past. Each day with Sofia and her family I had asked many questions, and Sofia was growing more impatient because I was asking too many questions about her, her deceased brother, and our mother.

"You must live in the present," she insisted.

I argued, "To live in the present peacefully, one must understand the past." Sofia disagreed, but I went on, "Knowing my past in Germany is helping me in the present."

The conversation between us was becoming more heated. I could see that my half-sister and I were much alike in our lives and in our stubbornness. "No, forget the past! Just live today." As she talked, I stared into her eyes and fell back to the times that I had dreamed of being with my birth mother. A parade of all my childhood and adult antics marched to the beat of Sofia's clipped voice--stealing money to give to the missions, wetting the bed, pretending to be a master pianist, having an imaginary boyfriend who was killed in the Viet Nam War, feigning a blackout, playacting as a highly regarded hero, and various versions of refusing to let people into my life. "Marita . . . Marita? Forget the past. Just live today!"

I quickly shifted my eyes from Sofia to my mother's living room window. She was observing our wild hand gestures and animated facial expressions, her two daughters together.

We walked into my mother's house. This time Aunt Birgit, my mother's sister-in-law--Sofia's ersatz mother--was also present. Again, I asked my mother's consent to talk in front of her other family members, and she agreed. My mother never asked me any questions, but I later realized that she had learned about me from Sister Sopatra and my lost letters.

Aunt Birgit asked my mother, "Why didn't you tell us about Marita?"

Mother repeated, "I was ashamed, not that I was pregnant with Brunhilde, but that I had given her up." I caught her slip of words. Did that mean she has wondered about me all these years? She also answered my childhood question. She was not ashamed of me.

"My parents were ashamed that I was pregnant, and after she was born, my father did not allow my daughter outside the house with the other children. He forbade her to be on the first floor. Marita was confined to living upstairs in a bedroom."

My mother, who had blue-gray eyes and red hair before it turned mouse gray, continued, "My father also did not like Marita's red hair and green eyes." During the Middle Ages women with those characteristics were witches. However, when my grandfather lived, parts of Europe still had a strong prejudice toward red heads. As a child, Sofia's son, who also has red hair, teamed up with another male red head to fend off the derogatory remarks. Months later, when I met my half-sister Sarah on my father's side, she recalled a neighbor in Minderlittgen bemoaning that her young daughter had red hair and wishing that she was as pretty as Sarah, who had dark brown hair. In England having red hair was called Gingerism, and people with "gingerphobia" often committed acts of hatred toward red heads. It gave me pause, and made me wonder if my mother was mistreated as a child because of her red hair.

In both meetings, my mother seemed obsessed over my father not taking responsibility for his daughter. "After I was pregnant with you, I asked Herman [my father] to take some financial responsibility, and he refused. His mother made him take responsibility. I took him to court to establish that he was the father, and, therefore, he had to pay. He was supposed to send money to the orphanage on a monthly basis. He said he paid 250 Marks, but he didn't."

I was confused about why this was so important to my mother, but I did not know how to say politely, *What am I missing here?* She was painting a picture of a man who did not want anything to do with me.

I asked questions about my mother's health and my medical history. She had a hip replacement, a heart pacemaker, hearing aids, eye glasses, and now skin cancer. Other than that, in my mother's words, she was "fine." She either put a new meaning to the word "fine," or she was a woman who could withstand a great deal of suffering without complaint. When I questioned her and Sofia about the kind of cancer and what was being done for her, I got blank looks. I asked my mother about the time that the FBI Special Agents came to visit her in 1993 to get my medical history, and she recalled vividly their knocking on her door. She remarked that they did not speak good German, and the communication was less than fruitful.

During this second meeting, I still did not ask any questions that would put my mother in a bad light in front of her family. I left with a void. What I took away from that meeting, though, was that perhaps it was better that I was given up than remain confined to the upstairs, an embarrassment. Later I learned that it was not uncommon in the village for babies to be kept in bed, especially during the winter. The rooms were small, and the heat was only in the kitchen. During the day they all were either in the kitchen or in the fields, and the babies were in the way. Also, keeping them in bed in an upstairs bedroom, and away from other family members who might be sick, was normal, but it was clear that my mother did not like that I was isolated.

My Biological Father's Truth

In the middle of my second meeting, Sofia interrupted us to say that my father was waiting for me outside the house, if I wanted to see him. Flippantly, as though I were saying, "It doesn't matter to me," I replied, "Yes, I'll take a picture of him."

How could I be so keen—no, so desperate--to meet my mother, and so glib and uninterested in my biological father? The reasons did not change; I was still under my mother's and Sofia's influence and my mother's roof. They wanted me, and my father, until now, had shown no signs of wanting me.

The translator and I walked out, and there stood a short, pale, wrinkled 87-year-old man with a cane. He had walked from his house to my mother's, a short distance of two houses and one barn. His walk to me would be the last time he walked. He wore a gentleman's hat, pale blue casual jacket and gray dress pants. As I stepped down the outside stairs, my first reaction was, "Oh, my God, you're so short!" The translator asked if she should translate that, and I laughed and answered a resounding, "No!" I kept my second reaction to myself; I look exactly like him.

We shook hands. We did not go inside the house because I did not know how my mother would feel about that. I still knew nothing of their relationship. Besides, my half-sister planted herself firmly on the steps outside the entry, and we would have had to tackle her to get into the house. Judging by the look on her face, it would not be an easy task. We talked in front of her.

"When were you born?" was the first thing out of my father's mouth.

What a curious first remark. "December 15th," I said.

"*Zu spaet! Zu spaet!* Too late! Too late!"

So, I quickly did the math again — as he was doing — and judged how arrogant of an 87-year old man to come to me after 59 years to acknowledge that he was my father, but to deny it when he finally faced me. There was no doubt that each of us knew he was my father, and I was his daughter.

"Come with me to meet my wife and family," My father almost demanded. I sensed he was used to getting his way.

"No way!" I said, mistakenly thinking that he was married when he had the liaison with my mother. I imagined the suffering his wife would go through if she met me. I cast him as the bad guy, without having any real information other than misinformation about what transpired. I was adversarial with my father in a way that I wouldn't dream of being with my mother.

"Why not?" he retorted. Perhaps if he would have been less arrogant, I could have been less argumentative.

"Because I came to visit my mother, and it would be rude to leave her." Old habits die hard, and I immediately threw up a protective barrier.

"But we cannot talk here." He glanced at Sofia on the front stairs. "She was a bad girl." He made a move away from the entry steps to another location to talk with me.

"Why was she a bad girl?" Sofia got up from the steps and moved toward us. My father did not answer. Sofia returned to the stoop.

"Will you write me?" my father quickly asked. He could tell that this discussion was not going anywhere.

"No, you write me."

"You will give me an address?" I had no pen or paper, and I turned to Sofia. She glowered as she got up and went into the house to look for the pen and paper. Upon her return, I wrote down the information and gave it to him. We shook hands and said good-bye. The meeting lasted ten minutes, at most. As I turned to go back into the house, I noticed an unusual number of people walking past, stopping to look at us. I did not realize until then that we were the talk of the village. Inside I talked more with my mother, but I wondered why she did not ask how the visit with my father had gone. If my mother was filled with emotion, she did not show it.

At the end of the second visit, the translator and I went outside to discuss payment.

"I cannot take your money," the translator said.

I was surprised. "What do you mean?" She was hired at a negotiated rate.

"I have been a professional translator for years, and I have never been involved in anything that has affected me emotionally as this job has. Look at my arms, the goose bumps. You have met your mother after almost 40 years and your father for the first time. Your mother's story breaks my heart. I cannot take any money."

It dawned on me that I had been together with my birth father and birth mother for the first time, even though it was for only 10 minutes. Their blood was in my blood. I was momentarily dumbfounded. I recovered and insisted, "You're a professional. I must give you something." She finally accepted a compromise.

I moved into the back seat of Sofia's car. Sadly I stared at my mother, who had come outside to sit. She stared at me. I waved, and she reciprocated. I reminisced to Sofia's story about Aunt Elke and her husband taking me from the orphanage for the day to visit Minderlittgen. I was not allowed to leave the car, and I remained in the back seat. I wondered if my mother was there waving at me from afar, as she did now, and how I reacted as a small child, once again leaving my mother.

We drove away. I was drained. After a few miles, I asked my half-sister whether my greeting with my father was acceptable. I was clearly loyal to Sofia and my mother's prejudice against my father. I wondered why I was not affording my father the same emotional investment that I gave my mother.

I was jerked back to reality when Sofia said, "You handled him all right, except now you have a very large family." But my shadow family was smaller. My mother, father, sister, aunt, nephew and his wife were now real. Even though I welcomed all into my heart, I needed more time to process that my sickly father had walked to me. Before meeting him, I had referred to him as "my biological father, *der Samenspender*, the sperm donor," the same way Sofia regarded her father. After I met him, he became a human being, and a new dimension of light was brought to my world.

On the drive away from the hamlet, I asked Sofia about my father.

"I knew your father since I was a child. He came to the house and played with my brother and me. I liked him because he sang and danced with me, but he drank too much. The more he drank, the deeper his voice became. Throughout the years when our mother hosted *Kaffee und Kuchen*, coffee and cake, she always sat next to your father. When I found out about you, I loathed him."

Because I had just met Sofia and I didn't want to offend her, I didn't ask why my father had said she was a bad girl.

That night I returned to my hotel room, and went through yet another night of pacing the floor and tossing and turning. Surprisingly, though, I was not rehashing the visit of my birth parents. Instead I was thinking about my American mother, whom I had hated all these years. Over the years I had thought little of her. As I paced the floor, my hatred started to melt away.

The remaining three days I spent with Sofia and her family. They were gracious, and the time I had with them was priceless.

We discussed my mother and father very little because I did not want them to think that I was only interested in my parents. At one point, Sofia sensed that I wanted to see our mother again and she offered to drive me to Minderlittgen, but I could not admit to her that I wanted more time, even if we sat in silence together. I truly wanted to know Sofia, and I wanted her to be not just my half-sister, but my sister.

I felt crushed by time. There was simply not enough time to address my 59 years of existence. Not enough time to know my mother, my sister and her family. Not enough time to understand how I was also like my father. I resolved that I was going to learn more about my father, and possibly spend more time with him, although, as a guest of Sofia, I was not going to do it on her time.

My Mother's Gift

Shortly before I left to return to the United States Sofia handed me a gift from my mother, a rosary ring that she had for years. I accepted the ring much like I accepted my birth father — with reservation. I opened the small, wrapped package as though it were the compulsory exchange gift at a workplace Christmas party. When I first saw the ring, I flashed back to the awful penance the priest gave me when I confessed that I sinned when I had wet the bed, and the times when Michael and I said the rosary in hopes that a Supreme Being would hear us.

The rosary itself is a beaded sequence of prayers divided into five decades that is a tribute to the mother of Jesus

Christ. It's a contemplative prayer that soothes the soul; the repetition of prayer creates a tranquil rhythm that opens the heart and mind to the mysteries of Christ's life. The history of a rosary ring goes back to at least the 16th century. The ring is compact and flat and can easily be stored in pockets. Hence, the ring is sometimes called a soldier's ring, designed for soldiers who were at war and already had heavy backpacks and duffle bags. In World War II, while fighting on the Pacific front, my adoptive father carried a gold metal casing smaller than a child's thimble, and inside was an even smaller metal statue of Jesus.

The band is also called a decade ring because of the ten nobs or beads on the ring that represent each of the ten Hail Mary's. Perhaps my mother Mathilde's thumb felt the protruding crucifix, and she judiciously stated one of the 20 mysteries of Christ's life and meditated on the mystery, and then moved her thumb to the first nob, and whispered, *"Gegrüsst seist du, Maria, voll der Gnade; der Herr ist mit dir; du bist gebenedeit unter den Frauen und gebenedeit ist die Frucht deines Leibes, Jesus. Heilige Maria Mutter Gottes, bitte für uns Sünder, jetzt und in der Stunde unseres Todes. Amen.* (Hail Mary, full of grace, the Lord is with you. Blessed are you among women, and blessed is the fruit of thy womb, Jesus. Holy Mary, Mother of God, pray for us sinners, now and at the hour of our death. Amen.) That is the same prayer said by my adoptive grandmother as she sat next to me in the living room while I studied in high school, and the same prayer that the Religious of the Sacred Heart said daily while I studied their soft faces, deep in contemplation.

When my birth mother's finger was awakened at the crucifix again, she prayed a Glory be to the Father . . . then, an Our Father, and the next mystery and meditation, and her fingers "took off" again around the ring. Five times she did that before she finally slid it back into her purse or pocket. Did she find comfort in the act? Was she asking for something? Did she give praise? What she thankful for what she had? How deep was her faith?

The religious object d'art was not the first material gift I received from my mother. I've carefully stored in a safe place the photo she used to introduce herself through the mail, another photo of us from when I had first met her, and now the ring. I hoped that my mother was giving me more than a religious object, but a message, a reminder that she had cherished me while I was in her womb and with her during my first three months of life, and that she had suffered many regrets, much like the ultimate mother of Christ. Now when I think of the rosary, I think of what the Old Lady had said about the significance of a picture of a mother holding her baby.

As I twirled the ring and let my fingers slip over each bead, I found serenity, allowing myself to revisit stories of my life and to imagine how my birth mother's life might have been. I drifted back to all the times as a child that I laid down on my bed and stared at the ceiling, wondering, thinking, fantasizing, not because I wanted to be somewhere else, but because I was seeking the truth. Frankly, I grew very tired of being inside my mind, but it's different now, because much of the truth was unraveling. Now, when I am away from the ring, I find myself going through the motions and I am brought back to a peaceful place where my mind diverts to my mother Mathilde, her family, and my transformation.

I stare at the Old Lady, wondering if she is awake or asleep. "Are you there, my friend?" Nothing. I speak louder, "Are you there?!"

"Yes, I'm here." Her voice is faint. "You had a wonderful trip. Are you going to keep in touch with your German family?"

"Yes. I hope they want to keep up with me, as well."

"You seem different."

"I felt at home with my mother and sister."

"Have you gotten both sides of the truth?" she asks.

"Not yet, but for the first time in 28 years, since I left teaching, I feel passionate about something. I am passionate about knowing Sofia and learning the German language so that I may talk with her. I need to speak the language better in order to get both sides."

"Get both sides of the truth, yes, but also know when to stop looking," she iterates. The Old Lady is unusually quiet, but she continues, "I don't worry that you will get hurt by your German family, because you are already too cautious and have spent a lifetime building safety nets. I worry that you will not know when to stop seeking and when to start enjoying yourself."

"What do you mean?"

"Your goal is to get rid of whatever is causing you to be anxious, right? Do no more then get rid of the weight on your chest," the Old Lady ends. She is not clear, but she does not want to entertain more conversation. I sit at the desk, twirling the rosary ring, hoping that she will explain herself. Suddenly she blurts, "An ass and a lap dog belonged to the same farmer. The ass stayed in the

barn, where he had plenty to eat and was comfortable. He should have been content. Meanwhile the little dog was always playing, following his master, and living in the farmhouse. He was the master's favorite animal. The ass began to feel sorry for himself. He wondered why he was not the farmer's favorite. The ass decided he would do what the lap dog does. One day he broke from his halter, and began, as best as he could, to imitate the dog. Once inside the house, the awkward ass upset the dinner table and smashed the crockery. He then jumped on the farmer and pawed him with his roughshod feet. The servants grabbed the ass and removed him from the house. After the servants once again haltered the ass, they beat him with sticks and stones, and the ass was never able to stand again. "

I finish for the tired Old Lady, "I shouldn't desire something that is not fitted for me."

After returning to the United States from my one-week visit with my birth mother and the meeting with my biological father, I noticed the life-long sumo wrestler on my chest was gone; the top wrestler left without a retirement ceremony. Now it made more sense to think of the weight as a boulder that had been chiseled away, and only manageable rocks remained. I felt more accepting and patient with myself and others, including my adoptive mother.

Eleven

BEING CURIOUS . . .
NOT SO CURIOUS

Belonging

S ifting through all the emotions and information after my short visit was far more intense than snooping through my adoptive mother's bedroom bottom drawer. I studied the black and white photos in Günter Hesse's *Minderlittgen*, a gift from Sofia, Matthias and Rita, and I drew my attention to the period during which my birth mother had lived. She was born in 1921 during the Weimar Republic. The country was suffering from the hostilities of World War I (as they did after World War II). The reparation fees were significant. As a consequence, there was hyperinflation, and sustenance was expensive. According to Hesse's history of Minderlittgen, an egg cost 100 Marks (perhaps $20.00 in today's America); a pound of butter, 2,000 Marks; a pound of leather, 10,000 Marks; a load of vintage 1921 wine, 1,500,000

Marks; a piglet, 60,000 Marks; and a horse, 1,100,000 Marks. Some historians surmise that this hyperinflation was a natural invitation to socialism and Hitler; life was too hard, and the people of Germany needed a new idea and a new leader.

When Hitler made his first move against the existing government in November 1923, it cost four million marks to buy a dollar. The middle and working class people's life savings were wiped out, and the German economic structure defaulted. From about 1925 to 1929, Germany was beginning to recover, but it was short-lived because of the Great Depression, again giving Hitler another opportunity to succeed. This was the era in which my mother and my father were born. In essence, my mother and her family knew what it meant to be hungry.

Günter Hesse's photos of the villagers working together in the fields, particularly during harvest times, were most revealing. The workhorses pulled the wood hay carts and plows. The Holstein and Guernsey cows were used for dairy, meat, and substitute workhorses. Some of the cows clearly needed milking during their plowing chores.

Four pictures caught my eye. First, was the picture of two sturdy women with hand-sewn, print dresses that fell to their calves. They wore short, white babushkas, and full-length aprons covering most of their dresses, dark stockings, and either dark rubber calf boots or ankle length dark shoes. They were harvesting potatoes, and pouring them from a worn laundry basket into burlap sacks. The second picture, taken in 1941, showed my grandparents on my father's side, along with one of my father's brothers, manually bailing hay. The men wore typical long-sleeve work shirts, normally rolled up, suspenders, and flat hats. The third picture was of my father's house adjoined on both sides to barns more than 200 years old, one dating back to the 1600s.

The fourth photograph, perhaps the most beloved, is a picture pf my sister Sofia, taken when she was about seven years old. She was a pretty, blonde girl in a long, light print dress and white knee socks. She stood between our grandmother, who was holding a Guernsey and two Holsteins, and our grandfather. They looked very much like my American grandmother and grandfather, both sets wearing traditional, German farming attire. At the time the picture was taken, I was two years old and still in the Frankfurt orphanage.

A week after I returned from Germany I received an e-mail from my father's son, Heinrich, and his wife:

Dear Marita Malone,

What a big surprise. My wife and I heard a day before your visit in Minderlittgen the first time from your existence. We were disappointed and sad to have heard from you only because this secret could not be kept anymore. It is strange to hear about a half-sister from whom I never knew something. This was a great secret of our father for a very long time, but the time unearths the truth. It is a great pity that we could not become acquainted with you. My wife and I would like to have contact to you, if you also liked this. We're very sorry that we could know nothing about each other or should know. . . .Also from my sister Sarah we are supposed to greet.

Another note from Heinrich and his wife's daughter followed:

hello dear unknown aunt.

I'm Vanessa, Heinrich's daughter. It was a pleasant surprise
for us to hear about you. It's a pity that it didn't happen earlier. . .

Many people in the village knew about me as an infant, except
for the people who mattered: my half-brothers and -sisters. With
the exception of Sofia, they had learned about me the day before
I visited my mother in Minderlittgen in 2010. My father finally
told them.

I also received a letter from my mother (translated):

It was a great joy for me to see again my daughter. . . . It makes
me happy that you were welcomed [in Germany], and that remains so. . . . I think of you daily, and I am grateful to Sofia and
Matthias for finding you. . . .You are always cordially welcome.

I have much wrong in my life that I must now repent for.
Your Mother Mathilde

I responded to her letter with a quote from Eleanor Roosevelt,
"One does what one must." My mother did the best she could,
given the times and the circumstances, and I never judged her.

*The Old Lady weakly jumps in, "That's not true. You judged
her when you were a child. In fact, you spent most of your life*

*feeling like you were not wanted. Would you have written the same
note had you not met your mother the first time in the '70s?"*

"You keep me honest."

*"You're also judging your father. What do you know about
him?"*

*"That's not true. I'm willing to learn about him. Heinrich's
invitation to meet him makes me feel welcomed by my father."*

*"And why are you judging your adoptive mother? The child in
you still lives that pain. The grown up in you must address that, as
well," said the fading Old Lady.*

*Defensively I respond, "I'm not judging my birth mother
for the act of giving me away—one act. I have judged my adoptive mother based on many acts combined. But as I learn more
about my German mother, my judgment towards my adoptive
mother is softening."*

Through e-mails, Heinrich's wife Karla provided information
about my father and the other family members. My father had
been a difficult man. Karla confirmed he was an alcoholic. She
clarified that he did not marry until 1955, and their first child was
born in 1957. All these years, including the 10 minutes I spent
with my father, I had mistakenly believed that he was married
when I was born. Perhaps I would have treated my father differently had I known that.

My father's health rapidly deteriorated after our first and only
meeting. Karla wrote that he has been a man of nine lives, managing to cheat death several times during World War II, surviving

accidents, and outlasting deadly diseases. I considered turning around and going back to Germany, just to know my father better and to let him know that I appreciated his coming to me, but I did not know how I would have been received by his wife and children, especially now that he was dying. Maybe seeing him just once was enough for both of us.

He died two months after I met him, and he was buried on my birthday. To commemorate my father's death and burial, my husband and I took an autumn hike in the hills on the Missouri River. My feet swished through the leaves, and I wondered if my father was one of those fallen leaves. At the top of one of the hills, I rested and looked out at the brilliant yellows, golds, and oranges, and pondered over those brief minutes with him. I was grateful to have them. I was even more grateful that he had made the herculean effort to see me.

On the same day as my father's burial, I sent flowers to my mother Mathilde, and my mother sent me my first birthday card.

> *"It seems," said the Old Lady, "that your shadow family gets smaller with each passing day. And with each day you seem more content . . . even happy."*
>
> *"It seems," I add, "that with each passing day, I am belonging."*

The one-week trip in August 2010 was the first of many longer trips. I returned in December 2010 for another week, knowing that my mother was dying. In 2011 and 2012 I resided in the area of Wittlich for two months each year, and from 2013 through 2016 I was there for one month each year. My visits were only in the Mosel and Eifel regions, with my two families. The information that I had received while on my extended trips filled in a lot of the blanks in my history. The trips were not separate trips, but a part of my larger journey to get rid of the weight on my chest. As I spent more time with them, the heavy rocks that replaced the sumo wrestler were also all but gone.

Oje, Oje

Sofia also sent me e-mails, reports on our mother's health. She was failing, having vision problems because of the surgery, undergoing more surgery, having radiation, and suffering from the humiliation of being old, sick, and deformed. I was yearning to see her again. My husband and I made hurried plans to return to Germany for the week after Christmas, four months after my first visit. This time I scheduled a couple hours with her every day.

On the first day, I met with Sofia and the translator at a nursing home, where my mother was temporarily staying. My mother and I talked more about her family when she was a child. Her father lived to be an old man, but her mother died relatively young. Her brother Josef, who was in the German military, was killed in World War II. Josef and my father were friends. My questions were still guarded, but I knew that I would soon have to ask her the burning questions.

"Did you like my father?" I ventured.

"No," she responded emphatically.

"Why not?" It seemed I had a more successful chance of interrogating a hardened criminal than questioning my weak, soft-spoken mother.

"He was no good." Then why would you sit next to him while having coffee and cake?

For some reason, the conversation changed, and we started talking about something else. I could not get past my own obstacle of not wanting to offend my mother or Sofia.

The next few days I went alone to meet my mother Mathilde. My only companions were a small German dictionary, a pen and a pad of paper. We managed to speak, despite the obvious language barrier. She told me about her sister Elke, and about her grandchildren and their children. She was sad that they never visited her, and bemoaned the familial rifts with Sofia. The rift was over her giving the house to her son. The strife worsened when her son died prematurely, and his children inherited her home. My mother repeated over and over again, "*Oje, Oje,* [an expression of disappointment] *das Haus, das Haus. Oh, das Haus,* the house, the house. Oh, the house." She realized that she made a mistake. I said nothing.

My mother acted according to her times, giving the house to the male child. My sister, though, was raised in different times. When all one has is a paid-for house, the value of that house — in the minds of the family members — increases exponentially and means so much more. Perhaps the historical house and barn together were worth 30,000 to 40,000 Euros, which in 2010 equated to approximately $40,000 to $50,000. In this case, because my mother's only possession was the house, she essentially disinherited Sofia. Coincidentally, although my American mother did not completely disinherit me, she, too, made a strong statement. The things that our parents leave to us are a symbol of how much they love us. I knew the anger and hurt in Sofia's heart.

On one of my other daily visits to my mother, I learned about my middle name, Beata, which was retained from my original name in Germany. At Sofia's and my birth, the tradition was to use the grandmother's first name as the middle name of the newborn girl. Sharing the same name with my sister was in itself a gift, to be part of her and my mother's mother.

"Why did my father say that Sofia was a bad girl?" I finally asked, albeit abruptly.

Without having to think about the question, my mother Mathilde said, "Sofia always spoke the truth. She knew that my father was not a good man."

"Is Sofia good to you?"

"Sofia had been very good to me." I was relieved to hear that. I wanted my sister to be a good woman.

I wondered what was going through what seemed to be my mother's uncomplicated mind, but I was not afraid to sit in silence with her. It gave me time to feel what it was like to be in the same room as she and enjoy being mother and daughter.

On the last day before my husband and I were to leave, I again invited the translator. At this visit there were only my husband, the translator, my mother and I. If I did not ask the hard questions now, I would probably miss the last opportunity.

I asked, "Mother, do you want to continue to live?"

"*Oje,* I am not ready to go yet."

"Tell me about your happy times."

"Oh, I imagine my happiest times were when I was a child."

Were you happy when you had children?"

"Yes, but it was a very difficult time for me. I was raising my children in a difficult time."

"How did you meet your [first] husband?"

"The Austrian soldiers were based in our village, and they helped the villagers to plant and harvest the crops. One of those men became my husband."

"Why did you and your husband separate?"

"After the war was over, he got a job in Cologne, and I joined him, but we returned to the village on the weekends. Eventually, Germany required all the former Austrian soldiers to return to their country. My parents would not allow me to go with him."

"But you had two children by him."

"*Oje, Oje,* but my mother would not let me go. They needed someone to work in the fields. It was very, very difficult."

"How did you meet *my* father?"

"He always lived in my village, and he used to come to the house to play cards with my brother. One night he did not play cards." Her answer seemed typical of other German women who were asked about what happened during a time of shame: stories so short that they were barely stories at all. I decided not to ask, "Was it an ongoing affair? Did you love him?" I am sorry I did not, because later I received mixed messages from both families about my parents' relationship. My mother was not a conversationalist; if I did not ask the right questions, I would not get answers.

During that Christmas visit, Michael and I met my father's second son Heinrich, Karla and their children. Karla and Heinrich did not know how to receive us — hugs or handshakes, but we quelled that concern. Our greetings were warm. We hugged and it seemed to put them at ease. We drank nine bottles of wine in a six-hour period. My brother was very relaxed. We laughed a lot and talked about nothing serious, although he said that on the first visit to my mother's house, he had deliberately walked up and down my mother's street several times to get a glimpse of me.

While my mother Mathilde was temporarily in the nursing facility, Sofia gave us a tour of our mother's house and barn. The walls were more than 20 inches thick. Prior to installing indoor plumbing in 1976, my mother was still using the well and an outhouse in the barn. Electricity was also an add-on, and one could see the electrical lines throughout the house, although they were stapled to the ceiling and painted over numerous times. The rooms were very small, each having a window. The entry doors to the bedrooms were early 1800s. The cellar door had not been opened in years and through time had sealed itself. We broke the seal and saw spider webs that must have been there for twenty years. Not being a fan of spider or cobwebs, I only looked down into a dark, dank room, which was the room where my family stayed when the American soldiers sequestered their house.

We then toured the barn. Sofia told stories about how poor they had been. She hardly took a breath between stories. "Our bath water was first used to wash the potatoes, and then for the pigs to drink, and then it was our turn. The entire family shared the same water for bathing.

"Our toilet paper was from the corn stalks. Scratchy and uncomfortable.

"In front of our house was the pile of dung from the cows and the horses. We saved it because it was good fertilizer. Horse dung was the best. It stunk, depending on the direction of the breeze. When the breeze went into the house, one could gag at the odor, but the family was used to it.

"Once we had no shoes to go to school, and our mother was too proud to ask for them.

"Our mother worked all the time, but she always was home to cook something for us, to make sure we ate something. When I worked and came home in the evenings, she cooked for me."

After knowing Sofia for a while, I observed traits that show fears of not having enough to eat or having a decent roof over her head. Sofia makes sure that her plate is clean. I could have put the plate away without washing it. She is thrifty and throws away very little. Her mind is "street smart" — quick and logical.

On New Year's Eve, a day before Michael and I were returning to the United States, I made the last stop to say good-bye to my mother. I knew I would never see her again, but I hoped mightily that I was wrong. As I stared into her worn eyes, time stopped. I let go of that hope. My mind was not racing through the past or the future, not making judgments or commentary. I had only one thought: an awareness that I was my mother's daughter.

As I was about to open the door to leave her, I flashed back to 1974 when my mother was at the Dudweiler train station, and she walked back to me tell me that that she was at peace. This time I walked back to my mother.

I kissed her on her cheek. "Your face is beautiful," I whispered in her ear. "I don't want to leave you."

I waited for a second, as I looked into her sickly, watery eyes, and finally said, "I am now at peace."

Forgiving Your Mother

While planning for my first two-month trip to Germany, I waited anxiously for Sofia's e-mails that dutifully reported the rapid deterioration of our mother. When my sister wrote that our mother was becoming cranky and verbally abusive to the male Polish caretaker, I realized death was around the corner. The Polish caretaker suggested that the doctor give her something to make her less agitated, and that kept her asleep more than awake. She was also becoming a bag of bones, eating at most a bowl of soup a day.

It was Easter 2011 when I accepted that she would not be living in time for my arrival in May. Sofia recounted that our mother called for me every night in her sleep, Marita . . . Marita . . . Marita . . . She also called Sofia by my name. My husband and I discussed ad nauseam whether or not I should go to her side, but I was torn about interfering with my sister and her family's relationship with my mother, much like when my biological father was dying. Perhaps Sofia did not want me there during this time. No one, except my mother, was inviting me to Germany for my mother's final hours. Finally, I decided to write a letter of forgiveness, to be read by my sister:

Since I met you in 1974, I have looked often at your picture that you sent by way of Sr. Sopatra. Your eyes and hair were like mine. Your skin was fair. In your eyes I saw sadness. In your face I saw a person who was trying to do the best that one can. We are, after all, only human. You worked hard all your life to put food on the table.

Throughout my life I have wondered about you. Before I met you in 1974, I wondered if you were happy and content with a family. I wondered if you had ever thought of me. After meeting you, I wondered almost daily what you were doing at the moment. In August 2010,

I was shocked to hear from Matthias that you were still living. I have told myself over and over again how lucky I am to get to meet you again and have you welcome me.

Now you are very sick, and perhaps tired. Your life seems to be filled with many regrets, and I have not lived with you to understand those regrets. I only know that my heart has been filled with joy to spend the moments that I have had with you. For most of my life I have lived with a heavy weight on my chest, and in the last year the weight seems to be easing. I believe you and Sofia have done that for me—what a wonderful gift from you.

I have told Sofia that I am thankful that you gave me away and thankful to my American parents for taking me.

What happened after that was mostly what I have made of myself. We, as adult children, decide what was good and bad in our childhood, and I can find nothing bad in what you went through with me. It made both of us stronger women.

I hope that you are at peace with your life and with me. We are all only human. I admire you and your life; you will always be an example of a woman who did the best she could....

My hope was that my words brought her tranquility. My sister emailed that our mother was touched and still, and then she said she would wait for my arrival in May.

However, my mother's willingness to wait did not last; she began telling the doctor that she wanted to die. One hears stories about people staying alive until they say good-bye to all who are important to them, but for her to wait a few more weeks was too much to ask; her will may have been strong, but her body had the final say.

In the meantime, I received a couple letters from my half-sister Sarah, the other daughter of my father. Not long before my initial visit in August, my father and mother had met each other on the street, and my mother had told him that in a couple weeks I would be visiting. On the first day that I reunited with my mother, my father and his wife had prepared a meal for me. He wore his best suit and a tie, and waited at the window, in anticipation of my arrival at his house. Sarah confirmed that when I did not come, her friend walked the short distance to my mother's house to ask when I could see my father.

Sarah continued in her letter that my mother and father were in love and were supposed to have married. However, my father's father would not allow the marriage. (Yet, Sofia contradicted that our grandparent would not allow it.) Even though my father married five years later, his wife was distressed by the continued visits of my father to my mother. When I look at the proximity of their homes and the size of the village, it would not have been unusual to run into each other frequently.

My mother Mathilde died on May 13, 2011, 16 days before I was to arrive again in Germany. Sofia did not invite me to the funeral, but she later told me that the grandchildren made all the arrangements. Nonetheless, I would not have gone. I did not want to interfere with Sofia's grief. I wanted to assert no "ownership" of her mother. If I had gone, I would have taken away from the funeral, which was for people to grieve the loss of my mother and give comfort to one another. If I had gone, I would have created a spectacle in the small village. Because one grandchild was on vacation, the grandchildren delayed the burial until the day before I arrived in Germany.

I was somber when I learned of my mother's death. I got the news early in the morning, and I continued to dress for work. The next few days were also solemn, but at night, alone in bed, I allowed myself to cry for a woman whom I hardly knew. I could not be angry at my mother's God for taking her, because He certainly gave me opportunities to be with her, but I wished often that I could have had one more visit with her. I just wanted to talk to her, hold her hand, and kiss her cheek one more time. I once again hoped that she would come to me in my sleep.

I suppose some might think that my story should end here, with the death of my mother. I had enough time with my birth mother that I felt wanted by her, and my compassion for her and my adoptive mother grew, but the weight on my chest was still not completely gone. I still suffered slightly from detachment and a feeling of being incomplete.

"Why am I thinking of the parable of the Prodigal Son?" asks the Old Lady.

"Because you haven't been thinking straight lately," I respond. "You're confusing your fables with parables!"

"No, really. In the parable the father forgives the prodigal son, but what about the dutiful older son who was always true to the father? He gets nothing for his loyalty. The good son must also forgive his brother. In this case, Sofia must forgive your mother. There were those in your mother's family who indirectly suffered by not knowing about you. Your mother was not completely honest with them.

"Forgive for what? Perhaps Sofia needs to forgive her mother for other things, but not for abandoning me."

"Yes, but you're getting all the applause from your mother for returning. How does Sofia feel?" The Old Lady rests. Then she continues, "True forgiveness occurs only at the end of struggle. You and Sofia have spent your lives with inner struggles. You have forgiven your birth mother, which means you are coming to an end of an epochal effort. Are you willing to also forgive your adoptive mother?"

I relent. "The more time I spend in Germany, the better I know the families of my mother and father, and the freer I am from anger and hatred. Whatever power was gripping my chest and heart is slowly being released. I forgave my birth mother, and, now I am able to forgive my adoptive mother."

After my birth mother's death, I wrote an e-mail to Sofia. I wanted her to know that if our relationship were based on the connection with our mother and not a relationship between two sisters, I would understand if she no longer wanted to see me. It is not unusual that after these first-time meetings, relatives are content with knowing who the estranged person is, without wanting to develop a relationship. That's a chance people take when they have these emotion-filled reunions. I, on the other hand, looked forward to having Sofia as my sister. I asked her why she had bothered to look for me, especially since she, too, seemed aloof.

"Because I was *neugierig*, curious," Sofia said.

I hoped that her curiosity would soon change into something more lasting, like caring.

Die Gemeinschaft, the community

My arrival in Germany in May 2011 was bittersweet. My mother Mathilde was gone. Soon after I settled into my apartment, I drove to the village cemetery to stand over my mother's fresh grave. I stood for a long while, wondering whether she could hear me and if she could ever again talk to me. I still had more questions that I wanted to ask: What were her fights like when she argued with her parents over her pregnancy? Had she wanted to tell her children about me earlier? If so, why? Did she, despite being busy surviving and raising two children, make time to think about me? Did she and I ever think about each other at the same time? Did my mother change after my birth and subsequent adoption? Did my mother share a similar angst that I had suffered most of my life? Would I be able to understand the pain she had when I was sent away?

> *"You assume, honey, that your new-found family is as you are." The Old Lady didn't want to speak anymore.*

The ultimate eighth question, though, was how important are those seven questions relative to how I live my remaining life?

I wandered a couple gravesites over to my father's grave. It was amusing because the gravesites are assigned on a first-come-first-serve order; if my mother had died just a month earlier, she would have been laid next to my father. Two plots away in another direction from my mother's grave was Sofia's brother's resting spot. After spending a couple hours perusing all the cemetery plots (many relatives were in this cemetery) and admiring the beautiful countryside, I drove to my sister's house to leave a message that I was in the area.

The next day as I entered my sister's apartment, Sofia immediately spoke in rapid German. She was angry about my e-mail, the one in which I allowed her to opt out of our relationship. She said that she read the letter several times, pondered it for hours on her balcony, and even telephoned our aunt to try to understand it. Because of the language barrier I did not understand why she was upset, only that she was. I never knew if Sofia had grasped the letter as I had hoped, and because I hardly knew her, she did not think I spoke truthfully about caring about her.

Sofia was also upset, because at the funeral, Heinrich told her that he was so happy that I was coming into town. Then someone else said that I was going to meet Sasha, the nephew with whom she was feuding. She was livid. I denied having any contact with him. Clearly she was suspicious of me and expected me to play by her rules. In a way, I was still her guest. However, after my initial two short visits, I needed to be with all my relatives and make my own determination with whom I wanted to affiliate. She had 60-plus years to make her assessments, and I had no more than a couple of weeks.

I made an exceptional effort to tell Sofia as much as I could about myself, but she did not reciprocate. It took me a couple years to accept the disparity, but I wanted her to know me. Sofia, on the other hand, did not want anyone to know who she was. Neither one of us talked about our grief over our mother's death. For her, it was taboo. For me, I did not know how to explain my sadness and joy in proper context.

My sister has been my first thought almost daily since I first met her in 2010. We share the same blood. The irony is that she is the most difficult to get close to because she is also a private, cynical person. Her family definitely did not show physical affection, and I initially made a fool of myself by hugging her and her family every time I greeted or parted with them. However, I stopped the hugs when the family members grimaced at each other at one of my "too affectionate" good-byes. At first, witnessing them cringe, I was angry and I felt my safety nets completely covering me. But later I realized that it had been my mistake that I had not respected who they were.

At the end of my first extended-stay summer in Germany, I spent my last evening with my sister. I left her house in the early morning hours, having tried to extend my time with her as long as I could. Eventually, I said an awkward good-bye and gave no hugs. I walked away feeling like the good-bye was lacking, but I also wanted to respect her wishes. I drove away, and after a few blocks, I turned my car around. I sat in the car in front of her house -- how wrong it was that I could not express my feelings. I sat for about five minutes, and then turned the car around again to drive to my apartment. Again, I stopped my car midway and did another 180-degree. I didn't want to be melodramatic or too emotional, but for once I wanted to be true to myself and do what I wanted. I also felt a growing disquiet because I remembered when Daddy, while in the hospital, reached out his hand for me to take, but I walked away. I remembered when my father tried to give me money to help me with college, and I walked away without telling him that I loved him.

It was now 30 minutes after my initial departure from Sofia's, and I finally ended up back at her front door. I rang her doorbell, and she opened the door. Without entering her apartment, I hugged her with a "Good-bye, Sofia," and she warmly returned the embrace, and said, "Good-bye, Marita." I walked away. Afterwards, I realized that she had spoken English to me.

It was not until the following summer 2012 that Sofia began to be more open with me. Unlike Sofia, my father's daughter Sarah and sons Heinrich and Adam did not hesitate to call me their "sister," instead of "half-sister." They were very protective of me -- kind, generous and considerate -- and I was overjoyed that they took me into their family without reservation. They seemed to want as much time with me as I wanted with them. With Sofia, it was a challenge. She, too, was protective and kind, but she always made sure that a wall was between us. However, toward the end of the summer she slipped up, and referred to me as her sister.

At the end of my 2013 visit, Sofia gave me the longest, warmest embrace that I had had in more than 40 years.

My father's home was very small. As the family grew – six children and two adults – my father managed to accommodate everyone. Unlike my mother's house, they had heat throughout the house, and they installed indoor plumbing in the late 1960s. My father's family suffered the same indignations and poverty that the other villagers experienced, although during the war, the villagers had potatoes and vegetables from the fields to sell to the starving townspeople who had no gardens.

The two World Wars wreaked havoc in the lives of the German people. Each village has a memorial either in or outside the church or cemetery. The memorials are not general ones, but a list of all the men who died. The old people still speak of their loved ones who died in the wars and who suffered. They speak of the escapes from intruders and hiding places in the villages. My father, Herman, like others in the village, had been drafted to fight in World War II. Had he not honored his draft notice, he would have been sought and killed by the German military. He served on the Russian front three times. The first time he was shot in the leg, and then his hand, and then his lungs. He carried the shrapnel in his lungs until his death. Toward the end of the war, the German military started drafting children as young as 12 years and old men. My father was one of seven children, and all his brothers were in the same predicament. His brother, who was sent to war at 16 years of age, was psychologically damaged because of his experiences in the war. Nonetheless, the German soldiers came to his parents' house to look for him to serve again. His parents had hidden him under a pile of hay in the barn, and had the soldiers found him, they would have killed him on sight.

For approximately 25 years, my father worked as a maintenance man for an American military base. When we met, he seemed proud of his years with the installation. Otherwise, I received mixed messages from my half-sister and –brothers as to whether or not he had been a good man. Although my father had a reputation of being a hard-drinking person, he also exhibited the willpower to decide to have his last alcoholic beverage and cigarette 30 years before his death. My father had nine lives, yes, but a cousin told me that when he died two months after our meeting, he had willed it.

I spent my summers in Germany enjoying a slower life. The area is comprised of mostly villages, all with their small meat markets, bakeries, churches, assembly buildings, community grill huts, tennis and soccer fields, and surrounding agricultural fields. The homes' exteriors are clean, and their gardens of colorful flowers are manicured. Between the villages are fields of corn, asparagus, sunflowers and wild flowers, vineyards and forests. Bicycles are common, and the trails are wide enough for bicycles and farm equipment to get between fields and villages. Every village has its own wine, church or village festival, music band, and clubs. Little parades pop up every week, and music bands from different villages lead and end the parades. The entire village enjoys weddings — wine before, wine after, and wine until the last person has gone home from the reception.

There is a strong sense of community in the small German villages. My brothers and sisters regularly use the word *Gemeinde*, community, fellowship, and *gemeinsam*, common, collective, united. During my summer visits, I regularly attended community gatherings, whether breakfasts, lunches, cook outs, festivals. My family gathered with other community members and spent hours drinking and talking with them. One of my brother's communities has a choir for girls and women only. A local musician composed a musical for the choir. Within the two-day period of the event, the entire village, as well as outsiders, attended the event. The mayor of the village made an introduction and stayed for the entire event. When it was over, people stayed and drank beer and other beverages, ate sandwiches, and talked until the early morning hours. There was constant laughter. I attended events in other villages, as well, and experienced the same *Gemeinschaft*. When one of my brothers asked me if Americans have similar camaraderie, I answered that the spirit of Americans is different.

Just as I am proud of my brother John and our family, I am proud to be part of my German families. They are hardworking, good people. They excel with their hands as a roofer, tiler, tire maker, mason, and cook. They are the foundation of community life. I think back to the Old Lady's remarks about my shadow family, and realize that my German families are no longer stars in the dark sky. They are part of my real family.

Sofia's Weisheit, wisdom

While getting acquainted with Sofia, I resolved unsettled questions in my heart. My sister, most logical and practical, was clear on four issues: live today and not in the past; be honest with oneself; be and not do; and appreciate my American station in life.

During my initial visit with Sofia and her family, Sofia was adamant that the past was just that — past -- and she no longer dwelled on it.

"Live today," she said, repeatedly. Sofia might have decided that I was living in the past, because she did not differentiate between understanding and living. Soren Kierkegaard remarked, "Life can only be *understood* backwards, but it must be *lived* forwards" (my italics). Knowing my origins and understanding why my mother abandoned me gave me a new freedom to be and act.

I argued, "The person who does not know the past is wandering in the present, making mistakes that could have been avoided. That person is burdened unnecessarily by decisions that have been already proven." I continued, "The present is very short, no more than a tiny indiscernible dot on a time line, and the past is a line that wraps around the world several times. In less than a millisecond, the present becomes the past, and the future the present, and the next second, it, too, becomes the past. It is not enough just to live from day to day, but we must know why we act the way we do."

Sofia lived in the present, but based on her actions, her present seemed to be an avoidance or continuation of the past.

Winston Churchill's remark about the future added another dimension to my quest. He said, "The further backward you can look, the further forward you are likely to see." In other words, we cannot live purposely in the present and future without understanding the past.

I continued talking to Sofia about my need to know. "Not knowing the past has led me to a lifetime of confusion, low self-esteem, defensiveness, and withdrawal. Most of my life I reacted to events, but knowing the intricacies of my past has now freed me to become a person of my choosing." Sofia looked at me and made a fanning motion with her hand near her forehead, as though I were crazy. It was clear that Sofia was not buying it.

I tried one more time to convince Sofia of a reason to know our past. "In other words, time is the passing of cause and effect, and knowing the causes puts order in my life and allows me to take control." I mused over the Old Lady's tales, but I used a slightly different strategy to explain. "Buddha was walking along the river with a friend when a child washed down the river. Buddha jumped into the river to save the child. A short time later another child was floating downstream and yelling for help, and Buddha again jumped in to save the second child. Finally, a third child was screaming for help. Instead of jumping into the water again, Buddha turned and ran up the side of the river. The friend yelled, 'Where are you going?' Buddha replied, 'Up the river to find out who is throwing the children into the water.'"

"And?" Sofia asked. She seemed to like playing with my mind. Sometimes I felt we were playing reverse roles of the Old Lady and me.

"It is more productive to find the cause than to deal only with the effect or symptoms," I offered hopefully.

Sofia looked at me over the top of her blue glasses, and once again said, "*Ich lebe mein Leben,* I live my life." She found the story amusing, but not convincing. I accused her of being stubborn, and she replied, "And who is calling the kettle black?"

Now who is the Old Lady?

For a couple years, Sofia and I went back and forth over delving into the past. Some of these conversations, such as when we were in front of my mother Mathilde's house, were heated. She was exasperated that I never had enough information to move forward to the present.

"You ask too many questions. You think you are still with the FBI." She said one last time. We were in her apartment, sitting in our usual spots on her blue sofa. The coffee table in front of us was filled with small plates of bread, sausages, and cheese, but the glasses of wine and water, cigarettes and an ash tray were the mainstays.

Her hurtful remark prompted a sharp response. "Wrong, Sofia, I need answers to make my life better and to know you. And I am inquisitive by nature." I stood up and was on my way out the door. Sofia made some conciliatory remarks, and I returned to the sofa. She never broached that topic again, and I stopped asking her questions. I found answers in other ways.

I wondered how much information about my birth mother was enough information. I still wanted to know if my mother had been a good woman. If she were, I could have more compassion for her. Neither Sofia, who sees the dark side, nor Aunt Birgit, who sees only good in anything family related, wanted to answer the question.

The three of us were sitting in a cozy booth of a restaurant in a near-by town, and we had just ordered dinner. Sofia went to the ladies' room, and I popped the question to Aunt Birgit.

"Your mother was not bad, and not good," the aunt said with finality. Her remark seemed somewhat dark.

"What do you mean by 'not good, and not bad'?" Aunt Birgit stopped talking because Sofia was walking toward our booth, and she had made it very clear that I may not ask more questions.

I asked my aunt again, only this time in her home.

"She was not a good woman because she kept secrets from her family; your mother did not tell us about you. She never asked the family for help when she needed it."

My mind started wandering away from Birgit's voice. How does that make her a bad woman? My interpretation was that my mother was a proud person who suffered from not only the shame of child abandonment and unsuccessful male relationships, but also loss. She experienced uniquely different losses with each of her children; she gave me up, her son died, and she was estranged from Sofia.

Both Aunt Birgit and I laughed about my mother having "men" problems; that did not seem to enter into the equation of why my mother was bad. As the Old Lady and Sofia said, "Who's calling the kettle black?" I've had my share of "men" predicaments, and I hope that no one said I was bad because of them, but then, I did not live through two World Wars in a small, Catholic, European village that thrived on gossip. She was a woman without a husband during difficult economic and social times. Nevertheless, do answers to questions about my mother that no one wishes to share with me change how I live my remaining life? That's the same question I had asked when I first stood over her grave and pondered my seven questions. If she were a good woman and did the best that she could, would I be less defensive or withdrawn? If she were a bad woman, would I be more defensive or withdrawn? If I have the power to change the rules of the game of life, it should make no difference.

I studied an early picture, which was taken at the time that I was born, of Sofia, who was about six years old and my mother Mathilde, when she was about 29 years old. I saw puzzles behind her deep set, tired eyes. Why didn't she disregard her mother's demand that she stay in Minderlittgen? It seemed to be a sign of weakness. But maybe she or her mother knew something about her husband that others did not know. Maybe her inaction was actually a sign of her strength. Why did she choose to take so many secrets to her grave?

When criminals told me stories of their bad childhoods, my unemotional response was usually, "Get over it." The Old Lady and Clyde had said that to me – the first, when I was a child, and the second when he told me he was marrying someone else. But why do some people, even after knowing their past, seem powerless to free themselves, and they remain victims?

The difference between people living in the past and those who want to know what the past is, is the difference between "getting over it" and knowing what needs to be "gotten over." The key is to know *and* understand. The management guru Warren Bennis (1989) said, "Nothing is really yours until you understand it – not even yourself." In my personal prison, I protected myself. With my new knowledge and as warden, I am slowly opening the prison gates to a world of free will. I am "getting over it."

Sofia's blue couch was always our meeting place. We spent hours in her apartment, drinking dry red wine – I more than she -- and talking about our life paths. In many respects, we had parallel lives. Both of us are independent, hard-working, practical, and stubborn. Both of us are ambitious and stifled by the societal norm that sons were the favored children. We are thrifty, aloof, and outspoken. As children, we were isolated, and now we are both content being independent, unaccompanied, and solitary. Our mothers' parenting styles were the same, although my mother Mathilde was 20 years younger. We were both raised by flawed mothers who treated us similarly. Our mothers failed us often, but not intentionally. Both mothers wanted to be needed and adored, and neither one was. They might have been prepared for the actions they took against us, but neither was prepared for her daughter's emotional reactions. Maybe this story is about mothers and daughters, not about adoptive mothers and adopted children.

Shoes. The small, apparently disjointed thing, such as shoes, made a difference in both our lives. Sofia talked about as a child the traumatic punishment after not polishing her shoes and of having no shoes to continue her education. I write in my story about the uniqueness of Marvin the Martian's shoes, The Old Lady's broken, black ankle-tie shoes, my adoptive mother's Army shoes and not putting myself in her shoes, my American brother's Haferi shoes and I tying my own shoes at an unusually early stage in childhood. I tell a story of living on a shoestring, and I'm attracted to the shoes and boots of the German women working in the fields. Oddly, both Sofia and I have a habit of collecting shoes. She never polishes them, and I always polish mine. Even though my sister and I have many similarities, as a result of a small thing, we took dramatically different courses in life.

When I was an adolescent, the Old Lady talked about the importance of developing parts of the brain to practice affection, compassion and other emotions, and to feel a sense of attachment. The mother is usually the key figure in developing these attributes. I flashed back on my efforts to develop myself. Until my midlife, I gave others the impression that I was a cold person, but I taught myself at least to appear warmer. I studied and mimicked others. I awkwardly began to hug the people about whom I cared. I started with a simultaneous hand shake and hug, to keep the person guessing where I stood with him or her. When I was a high school basketball coach, parents and students knew me as demanding and loud on the court, and certainly not one to show affection. When one of the players became frustrated with her play, I benched her to help her gain composure. As she walked off the court toward me, I uncharacteristically raised my hand and gently cupped the side of her face, saying, softly, even compassionately, "It's all right, Shelley." I practiced smiling and laughing when others smiled or laughed. When people expressed sadness and unhappiness, I trained myself to study their eyes and fix on their concerns. Eventually my outward show of affection became part of me.

I also realized that control is only an illusion. I had assumed that if I had command over myself, others did not. I deluded myself into thinking I had control; what I really had was choice. I chose paths that steered me away from rejection and into self-loathing, and ironically, let my past control me; my past control me; my past gave me a neat and compact answer to my suffering. Essentially, I learned that I could change the rules of the game from when I was a child. I could teach myself to become whom I wanted to be.

Sofia's second piece of wisdom came from her repeated accusation, *"Du bist nicht ehrlich*, you are not honest!" Sofia is a woman of passionate honesty and loyalty, two traits we shared, but she challenged my honesty. When she first confronted me, she seemed to be telling me that I was lying to her, and I took exception to her accusation. But she was telling me that I was not being honest with myself. I was lying to myself about who I was. I flashed back to the Old Lady's story of the ass that died when the horse refused to help with the burden. The ass says of the horse, *"By refusing to carry my fair share of the load, I must now carry everything, including the dead weight of my poor companion."*'

Sofia, Aunt Birgit, and I went out to dinner in a Greek restaurant in Wittlich after a memorial Mass for my mother. Sofia was hosting it, and she sought out a comfortable restaurant where the Greek colors created a relaxing harmony against the wood. After we placed our order, Birgit looked at me.

"Are you Catholic?"

I became instantly uncomfortable. I don't like to talk about God. "Yes, but I don't go to church regularly. My husband and I prefer the Episcopal Church. Frankly, I got tired of hearing about abortion. And we got tired of being asked for money to pay for all the lawsuits against the priests. Hypocritical, don't you think?"

She ignored my rhetorical question. "Why didn't you participate in the Mass?" She was referring to my non-participation in the general prayers, not following along in the prayer book, and not taking Communion."

"I haven't for years."

"Why?"

I looked over at Sofia, and she looked as though she was waiting to pounce. Her expression looked similar to a cat's, with the mouse all but in its mouth. "I have an obstacle believing in the God taught by the Catholic Church. I was cared for by the Catholic nuns, raised by a staunchly Catholic family, and went to Catholic schools. But I prayed to find answers for almost 60 years, and none came to me. I prayed to be a better child and for my adoptive mother to love me; I assumed it was entirely my fault. I assumed I was unlovable. When she died, she showed her disdain by leaving me only 15 percent of the small estate. I prayed really hard for my father to live, but he died. I even tried to fool God by throwing in prayers of praise and thankfulness, so that he wouldn't just think I was greedy. I prayed a lot." I paused.

"It seems that in my life the only good things that happened were the things that I made happen, or that other good people made happen for me. My adoptive grandmother and aunts devoted their lives to God and the Catholic Church. And our mother . . . ," I pointed at Sofia, "Our mother prayed daily and often. All had a blind faith, hoping for a better life after death, hoping for comfort and peace that she did not have on earth."

Sofia stared at me, and Aunt Birgit put her head down to study the pomme frittes on her dinner plate.

I regrouped. "I believe when you're dead, you're dead. That is why this life is so important. I believe that you must do good deeds on earth and make your mark in this world. What if Heaven isn't what you expected? Once you're dead, you have no more opportunities to contribute to this life. You have to do good now. Improve *this* world. That is why we were given our lives."

Aunt Birgit was not afraid to take on anyone in any subject. She asked, "Do you believe in the soul?"

"I do, but I feel that the soul takes a special form. For example, our mother is dead. What did I learn from her? Primarily compassion. That is part of our mother's spirit that will continue to live in me. Hopefully I will be more compassionate to someone else, and that person will and be changed by it. Then, he will do the same for someone else. The spirit goes on from person to person and the name changes, but the spirit is the same. When I consider compassion now, I think of our mother — of Tilli's spirit. The recipient of my compassion will call it Marita's spirit, after I die. But essentially, it's Tilli's spirit that is living on through other people from generation to generation."

Aunt Birgit persisted, "But what were you doing in church during Mass while we were praying and going to communion?"

"I was giving voice to my hopes that our mother is with her God… the one that she prayed to all her life."

"*Du bist nicht ehrlich!*" Sofia just got her mouse. As I squirmed, she asked how could I not believe in a God, after what I just said to Birgit? Perhaps Sofia misunderstood my German, because I said "her" God, not mine.

Finding purpose in life is the third piece of Sofia's wisdom, but it is more complicated than the previous two. Sofia's frequent response was, "*Ich lebe mein Leben,*" and at first it reminded me of the beer and steak people, who have no higher purpose beyond eating steak every day and being able to afford beer. But, she also said her aim is a way to make her life simple and manageable: get up in the morning; sit on the balcony; enjoy the sun, sky and flowers; spend time with and help the family; and go to festivities in the villages. I confused purpose in life with doing something. Sofia's purpose is being.

For most of my life, work defined me. I have no children, and my work was my life. Today, if I were to identify my positive contributions to society, it would be the life lessons that I, as a teacher, gave to my basketball players and students; my example to other FBI employees about the importance of reputation and hard work; my sincerity and earnestness; and my willingness to help others. No job description refers to these traits. These attributes are who I am, not what I do. Sofia reminded me that being in itself *is* purposeful. Knowing that, I feel more free and accepting. I can now study personal growth for a higher consciousness, that is, an introspective quest for knowledge and truth.

To emphasize being, though, I must forgive myself for my behavior and thoughts as a child. The self-loathing, low self-esteem, detachment and other negative emotions were all signs of my guilt. Although I still have a ways to go before I have completely forgiven myself, my anxiety is gone, and I realize that I, too, am human, like Mother and my mother Mathilde.

Sofia's fourth sagacious remark was made before she met me. She told her son that I was better off in the United States. Before I went through this process of knowing my birth mother and the families, I would have strongly disagreed, because I could not imagine having been as tormented in Germany as I was in the States. I was resolute that in Germany I would have known who I was. Having a mother's love, regardless of the living situation, surely was worth more than having had material opportunities. But would I have been like my sister, who had the desire to do more with her life, but did not have the wherewithal to make it happen?

Sofia was raised in a household with a sibling, our mother, sometimes an uncle, and the grandparents. Although the grandmother died young, the grandfather lived throughout Sofia's youth. She never had a father, but she had a male model in the house. Aunt Birgit substantiated that during World War II and thereafter most people in the village were poor and suffered horrendous indignations and losses, but most of them recovered and have again taken charge of their lives. Sofia's family was poor. When Sofia married, her lot in life improved, but when she divorced her husband, she was again without money. Her struggle at first was like mine in some ways, but her struggle continues, and mine has ended.

Sofia has not talked much about our mother. I don't know how or if she grieved over the loss of her. For Sofia to still be bitter must have been more than an inheritance issue. My sister has described my mother as being cold, having little patience, and helping only her son to succeed, all of which are the same complaints I had of my adoptive mother. After Sofia read my letter of forgiveness to my mother, my mother said, "Good, I will live until she comes to visit me again, and she can take care of me." Sofia confronted her, "Why should she take care of you, when you had done nothing for her?" My mother was upset with Sofia's honest remark, and told her to leave the house. If that comment is an indication of my mother's true character, and not just the ramblings of a dying old woman, then for most of my life I have the proverbial grass was greener on the other side of the fence, when it was not. I might have been as frustrated with my life as Sofia was, and been in conflict with my mother, sister, and my desire to achieve. Had I lived in my mother Mathilde's house, along with Sofia and my half-brother, would I be telling a story about my birth mother the way I wrote about Mother? I cannot help but wonder whether my adoptive mother struggled daily with wanting to return me to the orphanage. Did she question how much longer she could stay committed to me?

Certainly the grass is not greener when I see the strife among my birth father's and mother's family members. In both families, the arguments are over money, affection, and fairness. The grass is not greener when I think of the opportunities that were available to me in the United States. In Germany, I am not sure that I would have known what those opportunities were, and I might have been a frustrated, bitter woman with no legitimate outlet. Even though I did not receive love and warmth from my adoptive mother, by virtue of growing up in and living in the United States I had considerable opportunity to improve my material lot in life.

I am, as a German friend had said to me, a *Nimmersatt*. Literally the word means glutton for something. I always want more. I always want to do more, but I was never sure to what end. While in Germany, I spent a lot of time walking through the villages and towns, and what might have been half-hour walks turned into long walks, because I kept looking around the next corner to see where it led. My wondering nature is responsible for my curiosity and willingness to seek answers. Until my most recent meetings with my birth mother, I had attributed being a *Nimmersatt* to my search for a reason for living, but even after my answers have been revealed, I still have that lust; there is no limit to my desire to want answers. Without that characteristic, perhaps I would have died with the weight on my chest. It brings me happiness.

Twelve

Arriving at Seamless Time

*L*ooking back at the experience of meeting my biological parents, I think of the missed opportunities I had before Sofia and her family gave me a rare final chance. Without Sofia, I might, at best, have been standing over my birth parents' graves, wondering, and still living with the weight on my chest.

Meeting them would not have been enough, though, to get rid of the weight on my chest. My German relatives graciously helped fill in many pieces of the puzzle by providing pictures and information. Having welcoming sisters, brothers, aunts and cousins, and knowing that they accept me as part of their families, made it possible for me to finally throw the sumo wrestler off. He is gone.

Knowing from where I came has made a major difference in my life. Although I criticize Sofia for not changing the rules of the game from when she was a child, I had not changed the majority of my own childhood rules until recently. As Yehuda Berg in *The*

*Power of Kabbala*h (2010) teaches, "We must question everything, and then make sure what we've learned is working for us" (p. 5). I now know that even if my adoptive parents did not provide me with what I had needed to be less of a victim, I was "better off."

After my return from my extended stay in Germany in late 2012, I decided to visit the old stucco bungalow, my childhood home. I parked at the car wash business across the street and stared at what once was the beginning of a long story. The pear tree and the stand-alone garage were gone, but the white stucco house remained, but not for long. The windows were boarded up.

I whispered over my thoughts, "How appropriate."

My nature is that I will never be satisfied, but the negative feelings of rejection, anger, and of being unloved are gone. Now I laugh more, and most thoughts are not naturally negative. I have let go, to the point that time is more seamless; the past, the present, and the future seem to be one. I have forgiven my birth and adoptive mothers, and I forgave the sumo wrestler for pushing on my chest. He did not have a perfect tournament, because I won the final bout. I am also forgiving myself. The journey was long, but as the Germans say, "*Es lohnt sich*, it [was] worth it."

My lifetime friend and companion, the Old Lady, is also gone. She still sets in her same spot, her back straight, her shoulders stooped, holding up my books. She stopped talking to me shortly after I said that I had forgiven my birth mother and adoptive mother.

"Thank you, Old Lady," I said to myself, as I placed the book *Aesop's Fables* against her back. I took a second to glimpse over my library and office toys and memorabilia. "Thank you, my mother Mathilde, for giving me away. Thank you, Mother, for taking me."

CPSIA information can be obtained
at www.ICGtesting.com
Printed in the USA
LVOW11s1444170417
531095LV00001B/308/P